THE BLACK TRUMP SUPPORTER

The Re-Awakening of a Nation

By
Gulf War Veteran,
Political Pundit,
Hip Hop R&B Recording Artist
"MICHAEL AMEER"

THE BLACK TRUMP SUPPORTER

Copyright © 2025 Michael Ameer

All rights reserved. No part of this book may be reproduced, distributed, or transmitted in any form or by any means, including photocopying, recording, or other electronic or mechanical methods, without the prior written permission of the author, except in the case of brief quotations embodied in critical reviews and certain other non-commercial uses permitted by copyright law. For permission requests, please contact the author.

Publisher Information

America Publishers
Email: info@americapublishers.com
Phone: +1 (617) 334-5774

ISBN Information

eBook: 978-1-966198-85-7
Paperback: 978-1-966198-86-4
Hardcover: 978-1-966198-87-1

Cover Design by: America Publishers

Printed in the United States of America

1st Edition: April, 2025

TABLE OF CONTENTS

Introduction 1

Preface 19

Foreword 25

Chapter 1. Michael Ameer's Life History and The Red Pill Moment 29

Chapter 2. THE REAWAKENING from Slavery to Salvation 70

Chapter 3. Donald Trump vs MLK vs Malcolm X vs The Black Panthers vs JFK 103

Chapter 4. "VENOM" The Vicious Blacklash Against The Black Trump Supporter 136

Chapter 5. THE KANYE EFFECT 152

Chapter 6. THE NEW ERA BLACK CONSERVATIVE STARS 159

Chapter 7. MOVEMENTS and MEDIA 167

Chapter 8. WELCOMING DIVERSITY 180

Chapter 9. WHAT DO YOU HAVE TO LOSE? 185

Chapter 10. THIRST FOR BLACK LEADERSHIP 191

Chapter 11. WHAT HAVE YOU DONE FOR ME LATELY 200

Chapter 12. THE KARDASHIAN EFFECT 274

Chapter 13. LOUIS FARRAKHAN EYE TO EYE 281

CHAPTER 14. THE BLACK BOOK 296

Chapter 15: TRUMP/VANCE 2024 (The Greatest Comeback in Political History) 313

Chapter 16. TRUMPS' RACIST TENDENCIES 324

Epilogue (A Bridge Built of Conviction) 348

Acknowledgments 359

INTRODUCTION

> "You Will Face Your Greatest Opposition When You Are Closest to Your Biggest Miracle."
>
> ~Shannon L. Alder~

The Black Trump Supporter is a political enigma to many. Observers of the political status quo and conventional wisdom undoubtedly expect any and every Black person to be a Democrat! What the onlookers have, is the misunderstanding that supporting Donald J. Trump is all about your love and affection for Donald J. Trump. This is not necessarily true, many who support Trump now were not his biggest fans and backers in the beginning. The landing of the Black supporters on the TRUMP TRAIN came like many everyday hard-working Americans, who supported other candidates in the primaries but seemed to stumble upon the charismatic billionaire and reality TV star and give him a second look and listen. Various voters supported Hillary Clinton and some supported Bernie Sanders. There was a war of attrition for the hearts and minds of America's voters. The ending, the last round of the Battle Royal, there, left standing were two political gladiators, Donald John Trump and Hillary Rodham Clinton. DJT seemed to speak more to the people, more to the heart, on everyday issues that affect American workers and voters. DJT was not your cookie-cutter conservative. He was pragmatic and "ANTI

EVERYTHING" you expect from a politician. What would make tens of millions of Americans pull the lever for this highly unusual candidate, let alone Black Americans? I will explain this in painstaking detail in the following chapters.

Blacks who support Trump or those who are conservative or libertarian-leaning have arrived at this destination via their own experiences, research, education, and pragmatic reasoning. This journey I call **"The Reawakening"**! This Reawakening is a journey of information, some over time and some instantaneous. There are many things today's Black youth and Black leftists do not know about their own history. This has been devastating to Blacks, that most of their history is skewed or omitted. In my humble opinion, an omission is the same as a lie.

These omissions have you stumbling in the dark, unaware of your true history and the ramifications thereof. Together, we will take that historical walk through some of the life-changing revelations that have been experienced by many Black Trump Supporters.

My history is rather interesting with many twists and turns along this dizzying path. I am a decorated United States Army Combat Medic, Gulf War Veteran, Emergency Medical Technician Certified, former collegiate tennis and basketball player, U.S. Army V Corps Tennis Doubles Champion, hit European Recording artist, radio show host, TV show host, concert and party promoter, US Government Civil Servant, and political contributor to The Populist Wire online news platform that reaches over 100,000,000 per year and now proud to add author to my bucket list.

My brothers from another mother; Black, Dom & Izz

My vast unique life experience gives me a varied, no-nonsense look at the world. Born and raised in Camden, New Jersey, one of the poorest and most depressed cities in America. Camden many times boasted the murder capital USA, top 10 or honorable mention. Still in touch with my family there and keep updated on news and social media about the city. The plight and horrific violence of the city, stokes my passion to not only say something but to do something. Many of us feel like we are just ONE PERSON and the powers that be will run over us and we can't make a difference. This apathy is the lifeblood of corruption and politicians taking us for granted. Rev. Dr. Martin Luther King Jr. was just ONE PERSON with a passion and desire to better the plight of his people. Frederick Douglas was one person, Malcolm X was one person, Harriet Tubman was one person, Sojourner Truth was one person, George Washington Carver was ONE PERSON. A revolution starts with ONE PERSON! Once you decide to act on your passion as ONE PERSON, you will find that your noble mission will draw many people along for the ride and before you know it you have a revolution. Like they say, a journey of a thousand miles starts with one step, one mission, and ONE PERSON!

There are many parallels you can draw between Donald John Trump, The 45th President of The United States, Rev. Dr. Martin Luther King Jr., President John Fitzgerald Kennedy, Malcolm X and Attorney General Robert Kennedy. At first glance, this statement alone would cause liberals to go into an irreversible state of cardiac arrest. Upon closer inspection, investigation, examination and a few calming shots of your favorite adult beverage, the door cracks open to let slip in the possibility that the men had more in common than most would comfortably admit. This is also a great part of the reawakening, coming to an understanding and realization of how past events eerily mirror today's. Unfortunately, many do not have the knowledge of pertinent events, let alone the situational awareness to draw common threads with them. They present a complex puzzle, but once put together, they form a very clear, precise, sharp portrait of events staring you in the face. This is when you will have one of your many jaw-dropping epiphanies.

Venom = a poisonous substance secreted by animals such as snakes, spiders, and scorpions typically injected into prey or aggressors by biting or stinging; extreme malice and bitterness shown in someone's attitude, speech or actions. A chapter in this venture I aptly titled "VENOM" because being a (BLACK), Conservative, Libertarian, Republican or Black Trump Supporter, there is no stronger pushback, aggression and attack than that, which will come from the Black Community. You may not know of this or have experienced it firsthand. Ride shotgun with me as I take you on this trip to bring you from that 30,000-foot view to look at that snake directly in the eyes. This is a unique and nuanced dynamic in the Black Community. Many Whites, of course are afraid to delve into this topic, as well as many Blacks and others of color, because it is a powder keg of emotions that could ignite at any moment. We have seen some evidence of this in public, as in the venomous reaction to Kanye West's political revelations, but still, some of the most vile things are private, in personal messages, back-and-forth arguments and social media posts with your everyday trolls and pundits. You will come away with a much better understanding and grasp on this phenomenon and its effect on the overall political debate.

"THE KARDASHIAN EFFECT" was sparked by none other than socialite, fashion icon and social media sensation Kim Kardashian. The premise of this effect is that anyone and anything can and will have an impact on policy in this very unorthodox

Trump Administration. This was also viewed through a very different lens depending on your political affiliation and which side of the aisle floated your boat, so to speak. We will thoroughly examine the pros and cons and the ultimate impact it had on **The Black Trump Supporter**. This also tangentially touches on 45's infamous declaration to the Black Community of, **"WHAT DO YOU HAVE TO LOSE"?** Never has language from the Oval Office been so coarse, direct and in your face. 45 now seemed like a .45 Caliber handgun! Shoot from the hip, kill or be killed. Maybe that declaration could be taken to heart by the MAGA man himself. Republicans in recent history have not done well with the black vote. We could reverse that aim on that .45 Caliber and say, "What does **HE** have to lose"?

Today, shaping popular black intellectual thought, we no longer have the moral courage and bravery of the Rev. Dr. Martin Luther King Jr., we no longer have the towering historical impact of a Frederick Douglas, we no longer have the fearless warrior spirit for black advancement of a Malcolm X, we no longer have the revolutionary ideas of a Harriet Tubman, we no longer have the intellectual largess of a Thomas Sowell. Today, sadly, shaping popular Black intellectual thought, we have stumbling rappers, we have mumbling rappers, we have going to jail rappers, we have the homie with the wicked jump shot, the homie gang bangin' and slangin' that rock, we have the boys trying to be men, their paths are fresh and not beaten. Today's supposed Black intellectuals are hard playing the victim card, leaving the black masses, lost, dazed and staggering in the desert, thirsting for black leadership. We will critique the metamorphosis of our role models and the crushing impact that it has had on our society at large and the tremendous effect on The Black Trump Supporter.

Not all is downtrodden and bleak in the Black Conservative political community. There is a light at the end of the tunnel, that piercing ray of hope. We are nothing without hope. That's what made Obama's campaign and its slogan, "Hope and Change" so powerful. All is worth fighting for when you have H-O-P-E! We always say the most dangerous person on the street is a person with nothing to lose. NO HOPE! We are now rising on the Black Conservative scene and have many fresh, young faces and talents. We already have many brilliant Black Conservatives, but they are from an older generation that may not as effectively connect with today's youth. Fortunately, we have some new millennial blood coming into the game to give the movement a boost, a powerful shot in the arm. This is very frightening to the current political establishment because the older conservatives have been rather maligned and contained, but Jesse, what do we have here? The new crop of young talent is connecting with a younger demographic, which is causing much panic and a new problem the establishment did not foresee coming. I will give you a glimpse into this exciting new wave that is destined to change the power structure in our two-party political system for generations to come.

Our inner cities encompass much of the black, brown and other minority populations. We are faced with a unique and very complex problem, politically and realistically. This is what makes the debate and the fate of **The Black Trump Supporter** so intriguing. We must point out the major problems within our Black enclaves. Then, we must come to a consensus on what problems have priority and who would be the authority in trying to bring about change to these problems. Here meets another collision of the Black Conservative and The Black Liberal. Problems that are seen by conservatives are not major problems to liberals and problems to liberals are not major problems to conservatives. We will break this down and identify the major problems of the black, urban inner-city dwellers and referee the tussle to see who gets to identify and implement those changes. This gets to the root of the problem, akin to a major clash of civilizations.

Blacks have always had white friends since the days of slavery, mainly the abolitionists. Today, we have what I call the new age abolitionists, whites in the media putting out conservative news, information and philosophy, helping to christen a new fresh batch of young and strong enthusiastic culture warriors fighting to free the minds of these mentally enslaved blacks that are trapped on the Democrat Plantation. These are dynamic personalities and forces of nature to be able to survive in the media jungle that is corrupted against the conservative. Blacks have been welcomed with open arms onto the conservative team. Many that are coming to the conservative side are getting a surprise, they are seeing a diversity of races, ethnicities, religions, sexualities, pro-choice, pro-life and open minds and open dialogues. The stereotyped, racist white man Republican is going to kill us because we are Black, has fallen by the wayside. We will touch on a few of these icons, movements and forces behind the movement to pull back the veil on a process the media is loathed to tell you exists. This journey of **The Black Trump Supporter** from the cradle to salvation is an eye-opening, positive revelation because we sometimes fail to realize we are more alike than we are unalike as humans. This will give you information, laws, executive orders and history that you did not or may not have known. You will be able to see things from a perspective you have not seen. You will connect dots that you would never have connected and if not in complete submissive agreement, you will come away with a much greater understanding of **The Black Trump Supporter!**

PREFACE

> "It Always Seems Impossible Until It's Done."
>
> ~Nelson Mandela~

Cigar painting from Red Wine

The Black Trump Supporter is meant to be a bridge between a highly misunderstood, polarizing, political figure and those who may not understand that figure completely, to those who detest them with every fiber of their being. The latter may be of course more difficult to bring to the table of understanding. The wide chasm that exists between The Black Trump Supporter (TBTS) and those directly ideologically opposed can be lessened by reaching out with common sense reasoning, facts and a true desire to inform with the goal of at least having that opposition empathize with your outlook. You may not completely win them over, but an intellectually honest person can at least say I do not totally agree with your opinion, but I do see a common-sense chain of thought that brings you to that position.

In this highly partisan, emotional political time of Trump, I thought it very necessary to use a long-form medium of a book to have people consider the views of The Black Trump Supporter. I felt this book is the best medium because you can sit down relaxed without an in-your-face or social media heated personal debate that sometimes gets so out of hand and emotional, little is gained in that type of transfer of information. I was mulling over this idea for a while to dive into this project, so I ran the idea by Jordan Farley, the editor of The Populist Wire online political magazine (to which I am a political contributor), and my girlfriend Lynsey (now wife), and they both said great idea go for it! Then, I began the tasks of notes and chapter ideas and formed the outline of this momentous project, of which I am proud. Some people talk, but I think it's more powerful to take some real action, so being a contributor to Populist Wire and writing this book. While supporting so many Black Conservatives and Libertarians is something accomplished, I see it as more tangible in this struggle of understanding the political leanings of TBTS and his mission to move the intellectual needle of blacks into a more positive and understanding place. I have been a conservative for about two decades, so I have felt the wrath of being called, Uncle Tom, trying to be white, Coon, Coonye West, an embarrassment, I don't know my race, I am not black, I am a sellout, etc., etc. so a literary undertaking such as this is quite needed.

If you are reading this, "THANK YOU!!!!!" I hope that no matter where you stand on your politics, you will come away with a greater understanding of the process of coming to be TBTS. Black Conservatives and Libertarians often are former liberal Democrats and there is a process of research and revelation that gets you to the point of being Conservative (The Reawakening). As stated earlier, in a heated debate, minds cannot be changed but if you are relaxed and reading a book, you can follow a person's trials and tribulations and walk in their shoes to have a greater understanding and soak in the reasonings and information that forms their thought patterns. Legislation will also be highlighted in this project to give you a broader overview of what has been done for Blacks in the Trump Administration as opposed to what is being done and highlighted in the Democrat party for the Black community.

Foreword

I am Dr. William Steiner, a long-term practicing dentist, pilot, writer, martial arts master, and editor for the news site The Populist Wire. In 2009, I wrote the book Stealing America's Future – The Unintended Consequences of Progressive Liberalism. In it, I outlined the post-modern decay, using examples and historical references, that we see in American culture today.

Through The Populist Wire, I had the privilege of meeting Michael Ameer. His ability to think critically and honestly are two characteristics in such short supply today.

Michael's book about his evolution to becoming a Trump supporter was a compelling story of his experience as a young black youth in a large urban setting, experiences that have destroyed the hearts and souls of so many black youths, today as they become enslaved to a culture that benefits them not. He discussed how Donald Trump recognized the problems in the black community and the solutions for those problems better than some of the most famous black leaders.

He talks about the empty promises given to the black community by Democrat politicians in their efforts to just get the vote. He witnessed the destruction of black families by the endless welfare programs that basically removed a caring father from monogamous family life.

He talks about the intoxication of young black males for unrealistic fame and fortune in the entertainment and sports industry, an intoxication that leads to no improvement of self. It ends up in anger and frustration.

Michael's book was difficult to edit, as I was so drawn in by his story and experiences that it was difficult to analyze in a critical manner. I learned new things from this book.

Michael Ameer's "The Black Trump Supporter – The Reawakening of a Nation" should not only be required reading for just black youth but it should also be required for all of our youth, as it exposes the lies told by Democrats to get votes and the lies of the media that supports those evil politicians. Our nation's future depends on our youth to recognize and cast aside those lies. - by Dr. William Steiner

CHAPTER 1.

MICHAEL AMEER'S LIFE HISTORY AND THE RED PILL MOMENT

> "I find that the harder I work, the more luck I seem to have."
>
> ~Thomas Jefferson~

I was born April 10th, 1966, at 07:41 am at Cooper Medical Center in Camden, New Jersey, USA, to my mother, Sarah Williams and my father, James Johnson, whom I've never had much contact with throughout my life, therefore of course they were

never married. My earliest memories were growing up at 2006 Kossuth Street in the Centerville section of the city, now nicknamed "DODGE CITY" (for the many shootings), which was a low-income housing area. Here, I grew up with my brother, two sisters, mother and at times my aunt, for which my mother was her legal guardian. I had an older brother, Roosevelt, who always lived abroad around the United States in various cities like Boston, San Fransisco, Houston, San Antonio, Richmond, Virginia and also served a few years in the U.S. Army and was stationed in Germany.

My brother Roosevelt passed away a few years ago from complications of throat cancer. Although much of our lives were spent apart, the times we would talk on the phone were very uplifting. His passing was sudden and devastating to me.

Band of Brothers, my brothers Lynn and Roosevelt.

I never got the chance to see him before his passing and that was a tremendous painful burden.

His passing focused on me, and I think this goes for many who have lost loved ones. This tragic sobering scenario makes you think so much harder about life, your time here on this earth, appreciating your family, true friends and your true purpose. Recently, the family suffered another loss with the violent passing of my youngest nephew and once again, devastation. Trying to make sense of it all, what I came away with in these dark times was to "MAKE A DIFFERENCE". I am only one person, but one person who is laser-focused can make a difference. This book and my relentless quest to be more than just a person whose occupied space and time will end up with me making a positive difference and standing on what I believe in 1000%. The truth and my mission protect me like an armor coating. Some may not understand my truth, my vision, my mission, my philosophy and my purpose, but that's what makes life interesting and challenging. The TRUTH is the ultimate judgment and reality. When truth is your constant companion in a political battle, you feel like the grandmaster martial artist, taking on a room full of thug attackers, and the old grandmaster emerges victorious.

After finishing elementary school and then on to junior high and high school, we moved to the Pollock Town section of the city, which derived its name from the earlier Polish residents of the area who were by then just a scant minority. While attending Camden High School in the spring of 1981, as a freshman, the 40th President of The United States was shot. I vividly remember this day, walking from school down past my former junior high school and seeing the celebration and joy on the faces of the ghetto kids from the horrendous attack on our US President.

This event would become a very important bookmark in my personal history and memory. This reaction from very apolitical inner-city kids highlighted the decades-long propaganda that has been perpetrated upon the Black and at that time, mostly Latinos in our communities by the race baiters, race hustlers, charlatans and government establishment. The only political ideologies these young children describe are Republicans are racist and Democrats are for the people. With this being drilled into your psyche before you could fully understand policies and the ramifications of said policies, it skewed your view of anything in the political realm. This is why I vehemently disagree with liberals, but I, too came from this neighborhood and this way of thinking and indoctrination, so I understand why they think this way. My mission, though difficult, is to lay out a succinct chain of facts that will get them to understand **The Black Trump Supporter** a little better. This will also get some more of those on the right to understand why liberals take such extreme stances on policies. This inching forth on both sides can theoretically bridge the gap and induce intelligent dialogue not the screaming diatribes we are currently accustomed to.

Throughout my Camden High School years, I can remember history and social studies classes teaching the trials and tribulations of our ancestors and their pale-skinned oppressors. In these lessons, I have no recollection of our teaching staff emphasizing that our oppressors were almost always DEMOCRATS! I stand corrected, for if at some point they might have pointed this out but I, and I would think many others cannot remember this being emphatically pointed out. These omissions of facts are tantamount to the cultural treason of our Black youth. The question then becomes whether this was willful ignorance or by design. We must realize why liberals have taken over the education system, academia and government. Knowing these sets of realities put together gives you an understanding of the power of liberal policies and how they are pushed forward by almost every established organization that we come into contact with within our lives. Once that light bulb goes off in our head, we see how liberal ideology flourishes amidst policies that go against the self-interest of Blacks and most American people.

Throughout my school years, I loved rooting for the Americans during the Olympic Games and watching historical documentaries, war movies and Black History. This gave me a patriotic streak and also made me want to enlist in the military. I also saw many people from many other countries, even oppressed countries, who were still proud of their countries. This is why Donald Trump's America First slogan resonates with so many people. It's just common sense. You always root for the home team.

The liberals want to make some convoluted argument that America is a stolen land, built on racism and everything is corrupt, which in some roundabout form or fashion may be construed as true. If these things ring true in a dominant way in your vision.... THEN LEAVE! There are planes leaving the United States every day. We all can agree that no one or one country is perfect or has a spotless record. There are evil and hateful people of all races and persuasions and America does not have a monopoly on that, although in 2024, we are racing towards communism if we don't stop this liberal freight train. There were many wars of every race, country and religion. There are good, bad, and ugly aspects to our history, but I will always stand up for the ideals that America represents. We fall short of these ideals, but that applies to almost every good organization ever formed on a large scale. The Catholic Church for instance, I don't think it was formed to molest young boys, but in man, there is an inherent evil in a small percentage and unfortunately, at times, a small percentage can infect the whole flock. The Police Force was not made to harass minorities and plant drugs on Black kids, but it sometimes happens. On the other hand, think of life without the good guys that are in the police force, think of life without police at all and that puts things into a better perspective. We, as humans fall short of the perfection of a higher being on a daily basis. We should be judged on our lives as a whole and a preponderance of our deeds should surmise our total character and contribution to life and humanity. This gives everyone room to grow. Life is a rollercoaster of events, experiences, knowledge acquired, and decisions made that hopefully will shape you into a good, wise, thoughtful and philanthropic contributor to society. America was very wrong about slavery, but this same country made its way to abolish slavery together with Blacks and Whites and went on to elect and re-elect a Black President, Barack Hussein Obama, the 44th President of The United States. I was never a fan of President Obama or his policies, but I did look at his election as what I saw how far we have come as a people and a country and that untouchable star that Blacks could always be proud to say I lived to see A BLACK PRESIDENT! But this presidency took race relations back decades. If you criticized any of Obama's policies, you were racist. If a tree fell in the forest, the Democrats would race to the microphones to blame it on racism.

In 1984, I am not quite sure of my first voting experience because I was not abreast of all of the issues, but I was an expert on the exploits of The Pittsburgh Steelers Pro Football Team, The Philadelphia 76ers Pro Basketball Team, The Louisville Cardinals College Basketball Team and The Penn State Nittany Lions College Football Team whom I followed religiously back then.

Camden, New Jersey (Home) Philadelphia
76'ers practice facility

A wonderfully PRIZED possession.

My political expertise back then was Black people vote for whoever has a (D) by their name. Jesse Jackson was running for president back in 1984 for the Democratic Nomination. Jesse swept Camden, which of course, was all Black and Hispanic. Jesse came through the hood and played hoops and back then, he was quite the hero in the Black community with his activism and proximity to the late great Rev. Dr. Martin Luther King Jr. I remember the opposition coming to our high school. President Reagan's daughters Maureen, Bart Starr, Joe Frazier and other celebrities are pushing for the GOP if my memory serves me correctly. Maureen Reagan spoke and as she finished there was a deafening silence in the room. There would always be courteous applause whenever anyone at an assembly would speak, but this was filled with a palpable thick tension in the air. During the awkward silence, one of the faculty started clapping and slowly there was a slight splattering of applause throughout the audience that slightly broke the tension. This let everyone know, you were in the heart of the ghetto and Republicans are NOT welcome.

My high school years were filled with sports, like intramural and church league basketball, tumbling, tennis, cross country running and every sport you could think of in the neighborhood. I became a diehard Pittsburgh Steeler fan and would play tackle football with friends in the neighborhood. When I became old enough to try out for the little league team in the area, my mother would not let me because I was rather small back then. Most guys on the field or the court would call me little man, this was crushing since football was the first sport I slavishly followed. I settled into tennis and tumbling which I excelled at. I was part of our varsity tennis team starting five that was ranked in the South Jersey Top 20 for the first time in our school's history in my junior year. The summers were also tennis-filled, participating in the Arthur Ashe National Junior Tennis League (NJTL). This league brought inner-city kids together to learn and compete in tennis, which was not a hot topic for urban kids at that time. There were very few Black or Black American players that were highly ranked in those days, aside from Arthur Ashe himself, Yannick Noah whose son Joachim Noah played professional basketball in the U.S., Chip Hooper, the big server from Sunnyvale, California, whom I had the chance to meet at one of our tennis clinics with NJTL in Philadelphia. With my knowledge and experience as a young Black tennis player, I would always preach that the feat of Richard Williams, father and tennis coach of Venus and Serena Williams was the greatest story in sports history. Raising two girls from the ghetto to both be arguably two of the greatest tennis players in history is miraculous. I rate this above Michael Jordan's 6 NBA Championship rings and Tom Brady's illustrious career.

The Arthur Ashe NJTL coach was also my tumbling coach in high school and after my sophomore year, I was captain of the tumbling team.

My coach's brother was a doctor, and each year, he sponsored a member of the tumbling team to train at an Olympic-style gymnastics academy in the much more affluent area of Cherry Hill, New Jersey. I was offered that scholarship one summer and attended the academy. This was a culture shock. On my first day, I instinctively looked for the next black face. If memory serves me correctly, on my second or third session, I finally saw another Black kid there. It was a huge, impressive academy far removed from the grassy hills and dirty floor mats at the recreation centers and schools I was used to tumbling on. I wiped out a few times trying new techniques, but overall, it was a great experience, and it showed me how hard it is to become an Olympic gymnast.

During my junior year in high school, I signed up to join the Army Reserves and my tennis buddy Anthony joined the National Guard. After completing our junior year at 17 years old, our parents had to sign the papers for us to enlist in the U.S. military. After successfully completing basic training, we returned to high school to attend our senior year and guard and reserve drills. This was called split option training, after your junior year, go to basic training and then after your senior year advanced individual training (AIT). I completed my advanced training in Ft. Sam Houston, San Antonio, Texas.

My (MOS) Military Occupational Specialty was at that time 91 Bravo Combat Medical Specialist.

My tennis partner Anthony and I got so much better at playing tennis in our junior and senior years that we were really expecting a full scholarship to college. Getting ranked in the South Jersey Top Twenty for the first time in history and getting a point from the State Champion Cherry Hill East squad was monumental. Cherry Hill East would shut us out every year in our school's competitive tennis history. My partner Anthony and I stacked the first doubles, meaning we were the number two and three ranked singles players on the team, but we were strong doubles players, so we played first doubles in an attempt to get a point in this match for the first time in history. We won a tough hard-fought three-set match and were flying high on cloud nine after that victory. The win was so embarrassing for the State Champion squad. The team joked with their first doubles players, saying that since they lost to Camden, they couldn't ride back on the team bus! We thought that with our outstanding performances and records, we would be considered for a full college scholarship in tennis. Boy oh boy were we naïve. We went to an all-Black and Hispanic school, which was a devastating basketball dynasty. The basketball team was so dominant in my four years of attending Camden High School I had never personally seen them lose a basketball game. When I graduated, our basketball team was 31-0 New Jersey State Group IV Basketball Champions. One day, I saw Denny Crum, coach of

The National Champion Louisville Cardinals at our school, at the athletic director's office. These are the recruiters that were coming to an all-minority school, not tennis scouts, as we brutally learned. This was one of my first lessons in life, about the realities vs. the expectations of how things should be. My tennis coach, who was an assistant basketball coach would tell us we had two advantages every time we went on the court:

We were probably better athletes than our competitors, and they would underestimate us because we were Black. We had two basketball players who had won the high school state championship together, Milton Wagner and Billy Thompson. They went on to The University of Louisville and won the National Championship together as The Camden Connection ended up on The Los Angeles Lakers and won a World Championship together. I am not sure this feat has ever been accomplished in sports.

My best friend and tennis partner Anthony and I did end up with partial scholarship offers from Rutgers University in Camden, New Jersey and Methodist College in Fayetteville, North Carolina. Since we were from New Jersey, we decided to take our talents to Fayetteville, North Carolina. There also was a pretty small basketball squad, so I was able to walk on The Junior Varsity team's second string. The tennis coach was a middle-aged, rather short, disheveled-looking guy, but very nice and personable. Anthony and I chose to take tennis as an elective which would be an easy "A" for us. The tennis coach also taught the tennis class. The team was so bad that the tennis coach could beat all of the tennis players on the team. He was so cocky as to say, "If anyone here taking the tennis class can beat me, you will get an automatic "A," and you would not have to attend class", which was great because it was a morning class. Upon hearing this bold challenge from the coach my partner and I, eyes lit up like a Christmas tree. We challenged the coach and both of us whooped him badly in straight sets. There was a changing of the guard at Methodist, #1 Singles was a freshman, a Black kid named Rod from Maplewood, New Jersey, #2 Singles was my buddy Anthony, #3 Singles was myself and #4 Singles was a Vietnamese American freshman named George from South Carolina. The first four spots on the varsity tennis team were taken by out-of-state minority freshmen.... AMAZING! We turned the team around to be a respectable competitor. I remember a tournament we were walking into and could clearly hear snickering, laughter and jeers of the other players. They assumed we were the same old Methodist College Tennis Team of years past. When all was said and done my partner and I lost a hard-fought three-set doubles match and were only a few points from winning that tournament. Needless to say, they were not laughing anymore.

In 1985, I ended up in Germany as a combat medical specialist after dropping out of college. The partial scholarship was great, but my family could not afford the tuition, which was rising so I decided to go onto active duty. I arrived in Germany and a white guy picked me up and brought me to my unit. I had tennis rackets on top of my army duffle bags. Bingo! Found a tennis partner upon arrival and we had a tennis center right next to the post. In 1986, I played in the V Corps Tennis Championships in Frankfurt, Germany. I was the number 2 for the Baumholder military community, and I forgot the name of our number one who played division 1 for Vanderbilt University, so let's call him Rick. I lost a close, hard-fought match in my singles and I was hanging around watching the other matches and waiting for my doubles championship match. I was watching our competition knock the cover off the ball with power and accuracy and I was marveling at how good these players were, Rick a laidback country white dude strolls casually by and I say damn these guys are killing it, and he calmly replies, "WE'RE GOING TO BEAT THEM". My jaw almost hit the ground with his matter-of-fact confidence. It took me four games to settle down and get into a rhythm, and good old Rick was right, we beat those guys in straight sets. We were presented with our championship certificates signed and presented by Lieutenant General Colin Powell V Corps Commander (yes, THAT! COLIN POWELL), Chairman of the Joint Chiefs of Staff and WMD Iraq debacle.

While stationed in Germany, I met a Muslim Brother named Harris. He was a great speaker, as were many in that vein of Louis Farrakhan, Malcom X and so on. He swayed us with his confidence, knowledge of history and captivating oratory skills.

We then teamed up to make an unofficial Black History Committee. It was organic, we just started drawing many guys in and we were trading history, religion and Black History books. Once this started, you could see a positive change in the brothers on post, who became more approachable, friendly, and seeking knowledge. Once this got out that, our meetings were getting bigger, some white guys were getting scared, and it got back to the battalion commander. The commander who pretty much called myself and Harris on the carpet and said we could not have any more meetings on government property, even though I was going through the proper channels to have an official Black History Club just like many other military bases. I was very defiant and hot-headed, and I told the fellas we would move the meetings to my house. They cannot tell me who I can and cannot have over my house. I was a liberal Democrat at this point and very radical. Before I could do much, I found myself shipped off to Iraq with a 4/8 Cavalry unit out of Gelnhausen, Germany. Landing on a cold tarmac on Christmas Eve 1990, trying to keep warm with a poncho on the cold ground. While at Khobar Towers between SCUD Missile attacks in Saudi, Arabia, I ran into Harris, "damn man, they got us both", and we laughed! After we left Khobar Towers many years later, it was hit by a terrorist bombing, killing at least 20 people in 1996. The war was over very quickly after months of Air Force bombings, and we were victorious, thank GOD.

I got out of the military in 1993 and still was a staunch Democrat. I remember Bill Clinton coming to Baumholder Military Post in Germany, where he was celebrated like a rock star. I supported Clinton even through his Monica Lewinsky scandal. I thought they were just going after him for sex, but I was more versed in Black History than current politics at that time. Around 2000, during Bush v Gore, I had my **REDPILL MOMENT**. I do not remember the exact moment because I wanted Gore to win, and something set me off with the Democrats. They seemed mean, nasty and evil the way they were going after Bush, his family and his kids. It was very off-putting. I was not too politically deep, but I was just following common sense. I felt the Democrats would stop at nothing for power. The longer I started to follow a conservative path, the more comfortable I was with it. Many friends and associates were shocked that I could support a Republican Administration. I was heavily into the music scene with hit records and MTV videos in Europe, so needless to say, my surroundings were very liberal.

I had the pleasure to represent the USA in Russia. That was an incredible moment.

Sharing stages with The Backstreet Boys, N'Sync, Blackstreet, Ricky Martin, Naughty by Nature, Montell Jordan, LaBouche, Haddaway, DJ

Bobo, Silk, Ja Rule and many other music superstars from the United States and Europe.

Late 90's on tour with KC & JoJo of Jodeci

Seeing my groups' names (Poetry N Motion/ Fresh N Funky) on Top 40 Radio playlists alongside people like Madonna, Puff Daddy, Mariah Carey, Whitney Houston, Blackstreet, Janet Jackson and Phil Collins was amazing.

Made Business Week magazine for my long awaited return to The Republic of Georgia.

Michael Ameer

Enjoying a great tradition after a performance

I even hosted my own radio and television music video shows.

Berlin Fashion Week

This newfound celebrity status definitely kept me in that rarified liberal air.

Hosting my own music video TV show

Evening vibes Wiesbaden, Germany.

One day, I stumbled onto The Rush Limbaugh Show, and he took the complex and broke it down. Many things he would say over time would be spot on. That's how I became such a fan of his accuracy. He would always say, "I know the Democrats like every inch of my naked body". You would laugh, but over time, it turned out to be true. I caught myself binge-listening because I had never heard of unapologetic conservatism, and it just turned out to be basic common sense. What draws me to certain people today, is their accuracy. Is what they're saying true, believable and informed? Rush and his staff were unbelievably informed and accurate. I got many mental homework assignments. He would mention something, and I would research it and vastly start expanding my political knowledge. People would say Rush is racist, how can you listen to him? I would respond I listen to him for 3 hours every day and I have not heard him say anything racist or point it out to me specifically what is racist. Needless to say, they never can. You listen to the show and then listen to Democrats and the mainstream media lies about it. Their willingness to outright lie along with the media made these two (media & Dems) worthless trash in my eyes. They will take one short clip, take it out of context and then completely lie about it. With research, history, common sense and a huge dose of results and reality, I would escape the Democrat plantation, running as fast as I could and never looking back!

Fashion Shot

Chapter 2.

THE REAWAKENING
FROM SLAVERY TO SALVATION

> "Your own Self-Realization is the greatest service you can render the world."
>
> ~ Ramana Maharsh~

If Democrats had their way from the time of the Civil War, Blacks would still be slaves. This is an undeniable fact. This is a hard, cold truth like a splash of ice water on your face in the morning. Try saying this over and over in your mind, "If Democrats had their way, we would still be slaves"! Now, you will start to realize the very heavy weight on your consciousness and history that it has. This is one of the first steps in understanding a Black Trump Supporter. We are critically thinking and evaluating the status of Blacks and their relationship with the Democrat Party from slavery until this glorious day. This gives you a complete picture, a thirty thousand-foot view to allow your mind to process realities without the noise, confusion, pace, groupthink, distortions and outright lies of the mainstream media. Many will say Lincoln did not "WANT" to free the slaves as a way to negate the credit he and The Republican Party get for The Emancipation Proclamation, the freeing of the slaves. The response to this is quite simple. Would you have liked the Democrats to have won and kept you in slavery? CASE CLOSED!

"William Ellison Jr., born April Ellison (April 1790 – December 5, 1861). Slaves in this time were frequently given their first name by their birth month. William Ellison was a U.S. cotton gin maker and blacksmith in South Carolina and a former black slave who achieved considerable success before the American Civil War. He eventually became a major planter, one of the medium property owners, and the wealthiest black property owner in the state. He held 40 slaves at his death and more than 1,000 acres of land. From 1830 – 1865, he and his sons were the only free Blacks in Sumter County, South Carolina to own slaves. The county was largely devoted to cotton plantations, and much of the population was slaves. William Ellison Jr. Was a Black slaveowner. (www.latinamericanstudies.org)

"The Atlantic slave trade and transatlantic slave trade involved the transportation by slave traders of enslaved African people, mainly to the Americas. The slave trade regularly used the triangular trade route and its Middle Passage, which existed from the 16th to the 19th centuries. The vast majority of those who were enslaved and transported in the transatlantic slave trade were people from central and western Africa, who had been sold by other West Africans to Western European slave traders (with a small number being captured directly by the slave traders in coastal raids), who brought them to the Americas.

(www.latinamericanstudies.org)"

This historical information highlights a perspective that is never given to the slave history of Blacks. Blacks captured and sold slaves as well as owned slaves. When we come to the subject of reparations, there are going to be some Black descendants of Black slave owners, so who are their offspring and who will they pay reparations to? That is a complicated question. What current Blacks have suffered under slavery? NONE! There are some Black families that are very successful. Should they receive reparations? Why weren't we all held back? This leads to (D) Senator of California Kamala Harris. She panders to Blacks with the assumption that she is Black. She is slightly blacker than Senator Elizabeth Warren, who is Indian. This disgusts me and is a prevalent reason Donald J. Trump was elected. No matter what you may think of Donald Trump, he is an original, speaks his mind pragmatically and is genuine. Senator Harris' ancestry situation in PJ Media was quoted as: "Harris doesn't owe anyone in America, but does she have some mea culpas to make in Jamaica? Her father, Donald J. Harris (how ironic), wrote an extensive essay about the family's heritage in Jamaica at Jamaican Global Online in January, claiming to be descendants of a famed slave owner."

Mr. Harris: My roots go back, within my lifetime, to my paternal grandmother, Miss Chrissy (Christiana Brown, descendant of Hamilton Brown, who is on record as plantation and slave owner and founder of Brown's Town) and my maternal grandmother, Miss Iris (nee Iris Finegan, farmer and educator, from Aeon Town and Inverness, ancestry known to me). The Harris name comes from my paternal grandfather Joseph Alexander Harris, landowner and agricultural "produce" exporter (mostly pimento or all-spice), who died in 1939, one year after I was born and is buried in the churchyard of the magnificent Anglican Church which Hamilton Brown built in Brown's Town (and where as a child, I learned the catechism, was baptized and confirmed, and served as an acolyte).

Hamilton Brown was born in 1776 in Ireland. He became a sugar plantation owner and founder of Brown's Town in Jamaica, according to university papers, textbooks and historical documents. Henry Whiteley wrote a pamphlet entitled Three Months in Jamaica in 1832. Comprising a Residence on a Sugar Plantation," Where he describes Brown's views on his slaves:

The same day, I dined at St. Ann's Bay, on board the vessel I arrived in, in the company of several colonists, among whom was Mr. Hamilton Brown, a representative for the parish of St. Ann in the Colonial Assembly.....I was rather startled to hear that gentleman swear by his maker that order should never be adopted in Jamaica, nor would the planters in Jamaica, he said, permit the interference of the home government with their slaves in any shape. A great deal was said by him and others present about the happiness and comfort enjoyed by the slaves and the many advantages possessed by them of which the poor in England were destitute. Among other circumstances mentioned in proof of this, Mr. Robinson, a wharfinger, stated that a slave in that town had sent out printed cards to invite a part of his negro acquaintance to a supper party. One of these cards was handed to Mr. Hamilton Brown, who said he would present it to the Governor as proof of the comfortable condition of the slave population." (PJ Media)

We are talking about a very nuanced but brutal institution when we delve into it with open minds. There are new things you can learn every day from our complicated past. I never knew there were BLACK slave owners and this really took me aback. The left does not look back to learn and understand. They look back to punish and gain political power and use slavery as a wedge to keep society divided. In conversations with our brothers and sisters, let's see if the magic word comes up..... RESEARCH? This lets me know that you are interested in more than what's on the superficial level. This signals I can debate with this person and still respectfully disagree without ending a friendship. Rev. Dr Martin Luther King Jr. said he dreamt one day his children would not be judged by the color of their skin but by the content of their character. The Democrats have turned that dream into a nightmare. There is constant identity politics, virtue signaling, and political correctness run amok. They seek diversity for diversity's sake. No diversity of thought, opinion or political platform, just a rainbow of colors like a Crayola crayon box. Once they have the multitude of colors and preferences, they espouse a job well done, although in "OPINION", they are in lockstep like a North Korean Military Parade.

"One of the most important aspects of Reconstruction (1865-1877) was the active participation of African Americans (including thousands of former slaves) in the political, economic and social life of the South. The era was primarily defined by their quest for autonomy and equal rights under the law, both as individuals and for the Black community as a whole. During Reconstruction, some 2,000 African Americans held public office from the local level all the way up to the U.S. Senate, though they never achieved representation in government proportionate to their numbers.

(www.history.com/blackleadersduringreconstruction)"

Before the Civil War began, African Americans had only been able to vote in a few Northern States, and there were virtually no black officeholders. The months after the Union victory in April 1865 saw extensive mobilization within the Black community, with meetings, parades and petitions calling for legal and political rights, including the all-important right to vote. During the first two years of Reconstruction, Blacks organized Equal Rights Leagues throughout the South and held state and local conventions to protest discriminatory treatment and demand suffrage, as well as equality before the law. Did you know? In 1967, almost a century after Hiram Revels and Blanche Bruce served in the U.S. Senate during Reconstruction, (R)Edward Brooke of Massachusetts became the first African American senator elected by popular vote.

(www.history.com/blackleadersduringreconstruction)

These African American activists bitterly opposed the Reconstruction policies of Democrat President Andrew Johnson, which excluded Blacks from Southern politics and allowed state legislatures to pass restrictive "black codes" regulating the lives of the freed men and women. Fierce resistance to these discriminatory laws, as well as growing opposition to Johnson's policies in the North, led to a Republican victory in the U.S. Congressional elections of 1866 and to a new phase of Reconstruction that would give African

Americans a more active role in the political, economic and social life of the South.

(www.history.com/blackleadersduringreconstruction)

During the decade known as Radical Reconstruction (1867-77), Congress granted African American men the status and rights of citizenship, including the right to vote, as guaranteed by the 14th and 15th Amendments to the U.S. Constitution. Beginning in 1867, branches of the Union League, which encouraged the political activism of African Americans, spread throughout the South. During the state constitutional conventions held in 1867-69, Blacks and White Americans stood side by side for the first time in political life.

(www.history.com/blackleadersduringreconstruction)

Blacks made up most southern Republican voters, forming a coalition with "carpetbaggers" and "scalawags" (derogatory terms referring to recent arrivals from the North and southern White Republicans, respectively). A total of 265 African-American delegates were elected, more than 100 of whom had been born into slavery. Almost half of the elected Black delegates served in South Carolina and Louisiana, where Blacks had the longest history of political organization; in most other states, African Americans were underrepresented compared to their population. In all 16 African Americans who served in the U.S. Congress during Reconstruction, more than 600 were elected to the state legislatures, and hundreds more held local offices across the South.

(www.history.com/blackleadersduringreconstruction)

As the most radical aspect of the so-called Radical Reconstruction period, the political activism of the African-American community also inspired the most hostility from Reconstruction's opponents. Southern Whites frustrated with policies giving former slaves the right to vote and hold office increasingly turned to intimidation and violence as a means of reaffirming White Supremacy. The Ku Klux Klan targeted local Republican leaders and Blacks who challenged their White employers, and at least 35 Black officials were murdered by the Ku

Klux Klan and other White Supremacist organizations during the Reconstruction era.

(www.history.com/blackleadersduringreconstruction)

The complete Reconstruction period if followed along party lines, you will see a pattern, like Abraham Lincoln freeing the slaves…….he was a Republican. Abraham Lincoln was assassinated by John Wilkes Booth, a Democrat. Lincoln's vice president, Andrew Johnson, became president as a Democrat. Andrew Johnson was not well-liked by the Blacks who were fighting for their rights. The Blacks who were elected to office were Republicans. The Black Codes and Jim Crow laws were enforced by Democrats. The KKK was terrorizing Blacks and White Republicans, of course, the Klan were

Democrats. This is a very simple pattern to follow: The Republicans were for the Blacks and The Democrats were against the rights of Blacks. This was very Black & White, pun intended!

This period is a very important mental marker. Directly after slavery, we see which political party Blacks naturally gravitated to. Quite naturally, it was the party that gave us our FREEDOM. THE REPUBLICAN PARTY! This is a building block of Black Conservatism; it starts with the basics. It is not that a party is perfect because a party is still made up of people, and people, by nature, are flawed. We have flawed people in every organization and aspect of life. Some think they can discredit the Republican Party or my stance on it by pointing out wrongdoing by a random Republican. I can point out wrongdoing in more than just random Democrats. The Reawakening starts here and it's more than just pointing out flaws. We can look at results, milestones, and historical impact and results over time and generations. This is how I look at things. I look at this political viewpoint like a man standing before GOD! When we envision standing before GOD, we expect the weighing of the good deeds versus the bad deeds, and hopefully, our good deeds outweigh our bad ones in this light. As humans, we are allowed growth. No one person or party is perfect. If you compare the Republican Party Platforms against the Democrat Party platforms over the last 200 years......THERE IS NO COMPARISON!!!!!!!!!!

The periods after and during Reconstruction saw Black Congressional Representation completely Republican. Hiram Revels was the first Black to serve in either house of Congress. January 25th, 1870, the governor and secretary of state of Mississippi certified the election of Hiram Rhodes Revel to the senate. Hiram R. Revels was born on September 27, 1827, in Fayetteville, North Carolina. Revels was a minister who, in 1870, became the first African American United States senator, representing the state of Mississippi. He served for a year before leaving to become the president of a historically black college. Revels died on January 16, 1901, in Aberdeen, Mississippi.

Revels participated in the Civil War, organizing two black regiments for the Union Army. He also fought for the Union at the Battle of Vicksburg. After the war, he settled in Natchez, Mississippi, with his wife and daughters and continued his career in the clergy. He quickly grew to be a respected member of the community, known for his keen intelligence and oratorical skills. Although he had no previous government experience, Revels garnered enough community support to win election to the position of alderman in 1868, during the first phase of Reconstruction, before he was elected the first Black Senator.

When the Ku Klux Klan terrorized the South during Reconstruction, many people denied that the group even existed. They were the military arm of the Democrat Party. The Democrats defended slavery, started the Civil War, opposed reconstruction, founded the Ku Klux Klan, imposed segregation, perpetrated lynchings on Black and White Republicans, and fought the civil rights acts of the 1950s and the 1960s. In contrast, the Republican Party was founded in 1854 as an anti-slavery party. Its mission was to stop the spread of slavery and polygamy into the new western territories with the aim of abolishing it entirely. This effort was dealt a major blow by the Supreme Court in the 1857 case DRED SCOTT V. SANFORD. The court ruled that slaves were not citizens they were property. The seven Supreme Court Justices that voted in favor of slavery were all Democrats, the two Supreme Court Justices who dissented were both REPUBLICANS! The slavery question was ultimately resolved by the bloody Civil War from 1861 to 1865.

The Commander-in-Chief of that war was the first Republican President, the 16th President of The United States, Abraham Lincoln, the man who FREED THE SLAVES! Six days after the Confederate Army surrendered to the Union, John Wilkes Boothe (a Democrat) assassinated President Lincoln. Lincoln's Vice-President, a Democrat named Andrew Johnson, assumed the presidency. He opposed Lincoln's plan to integrate the newly freed slaves into the South's social and economic order. Johnson and the Democrats were opposed to the 13th Amendment-1865 That Abolished Slavery, The 14th Amendment-1866, which granted Citizenship to Blacks, and The 15th Amendment-1869 That gave Blacks the right to vote. All three passed because of universal Republican support.

During the period of Reconstruction 1865-1877, Federal Troops secured rights for the newly freed slaves. Hundreds of Black men were elected to Southern State legislatures as Republicans. 22 Black Republican served in the U.S. Congress by 1900. The Democrats did not elect a Black man to Congress until 1935.

When Reconstruction ended and the Federal Troops went home, Democrats roared back into power in the South. The Democrats quickly re-established White Supremacy across the region with Black Codes, laws that restricted the ability for Blacks to own property and run businesses. They imposed poll taxes and literacy tests used to subvert Black citizens' right to vote. This was enforced by terror, much instigated by the Ku Klux Klan founded by a Democrat, Nathan Bedford Forrest. Eric Foner historian noted himself as a Democrat in effect, the Klan was a military force serving the interests of the Democrat Party.

President Woodrow Wilson himself, a Democrat President from 1912-1921, shared many views with The Klan. He re-segregated many federal agencies and screened the first movie ever played at the White House, the pro-KKK movie BIRTH OF A NATION, originally titled The Klansman.

"When all of the efforts to enslave Blacks and keep them enslaved, and keep them from voting failed, the Democrats came up with a new strategy, if Black people are going to vote, they might as well vote Democrat. President Lyndon B. Johnson was reported to have said, about the civil rights act, "I'll have them niggers voting Democrat for the next 200 years". LBJ was also known to have said, "We have to give them (Blacks) something to quiet them down, but not enough to make a difference, i.e. "WELFARE" and various government programs. Now, the Democratic party prospers on the votes that it spent most of its existence oppressing. Massive government welfare has decimated the Black family, and opposition to school choice has kept them trapped in failing schools, politically correct policing has left Black neighborhoods defenseless against violent crime." (the inconvenient truth about the Democrat Party....prageru.com)

An alarming discovery is coming out of city schools. Project Baltimore analyzed 2017 state testing data and found that one-third of high schools in Baltimore last year had ZERO students proficient in math. Nine out of ten Black boys in Baltimore are not reading at grade level. A charter school, Baltimore Collegiate Schools for Boys has different, much better results and focused students. That design appears to be working. Since 2015, the number of Baltimore Collegiate boys who scored proficient in state math tests spiked by 60 percent. In 2016, nine percent of students were proficient. This year, in 2017, 14.4 percent were proficient. (Chris Papst, FOX45 NEWS, Nov. 9th, 2017)

How, in this day and age, can we have this massive number of students who are not proficient in their basic school studies? My answer is education and academia have been taken over by the left. The inner cities have been taken over by the left. The government has been taken over by the left. When we look at things from slavery until today in a comprehensive manner, we see almost everything the left touches is corrupt and disastrous for Blacks. We were not allowed to read as slaves, and today more than a century removed from The Emancipation Proclamation, we are not proficient in basic math and reading? I and other Black Trump supporters are looking at the totality of RESULTS! Many Blacks are looking at too many situations with emotions that White Liberals plant in their head that even pit them against other Blacks who do not think politically like them. Let's take out the emotion and think about the results. If we did this as a people, we would prosper beyond our wildest dreams. School vouchers to let Blacks go to the schools of their choice have always been opposed by liberals. In my humble opinion, it would lessen the money power and impact of the teachers' unions. You see from my vantage point, this has nothing to do with the learning and education of our Black youth. That is a fact-based result. Charter schools are educating our children better than public schools. That's a fact-based result. So why take the position of not allowing Blacks to seek out the schools that they feel are best suited to educate their children? My fact-based result is this liberal left-wing policy is keeping our Black youth TRAPPED in failing schools, thus perpetuating an underclass, underachieving, government-dependent Black society brainwashed from the cradle to the grave to vote Democrat and keep the vicious cycle going.

We have lived to see a Black President, but we are still in a mental slavery. We are contemplating flying cars in this millennium, but liberals are tearing down Civil War statues THAT THEY PUT UP and debating reparations for slavery that they did not participate in. You cannot win the 100-meter sprint looking backwards. Progressive means to be forward-thinking but liberals are always looking back to slavery to punish someone TODAY for what happened centuries ago. My fact-based result for this is the bad situation in our inner cities and schools for Blacks until THIS DAY! This is what has blossomed from this backward-thinking ideology. We must learn and understand our past, not re-live it. Many foreigners leave bad living situations in third-world countries and come to the USA and become successful and surpass our Black community because we are too busy trying to figure out how to UNDO SLAVERY.

Many of us (Blacks) are REAWAKENING! We are looking at fact-based results and applying simple logic. Why, under almost monolithic Democratic leadership, our people are progressing individually but failing collectively? We have many successful Blacks in all professions but as a collective, we do not have any power. We do not pool our resources (political funding/lobbying) and too many of us are not politically engaged. They say for democracy to work, you have to have an informed electorate! BINGO! Brainwashing, propaganda and miseducation seem to put us once again at the back of the bus (pun intended). This brings me to Donald

Trump's famous quote to Black America, "WHAT THE HELL DO YOU HAVE TO LOSE???" The popular phrase of today in politics is Quid Pro Quo...this for that. We GIVEAWAY our vote for NOTHING! A democrat politician yells racism, and all the Blacks throw their votes at them with nothing in return except empty promises. This scenario is rerun every election season. Juxtapose that with the LGBTQ community. This community has political money and muscle, and you see Democrat politicians bowing to their every care and concern. Diddy recently surprised me by stating that Democrat presidential nominee front-runner Joe Biden will have to give concessions to the Black Community.

There are many opportunities abound now for our people to exploit, professionally and politically.

We seem to finally have a segment of politically aware Blacks doing research and who are fully engaged in the body politic. Now that some Black Conservatives are emerging to boldly challenge conventional wisdom like never before in our recent political past, they are putting their support wholeheartedly behind the 45th President of The United States, DONALD JOHN TRUMP, the #MAGA Warrior!

Chapter 3.

Donald Trump vs MLK vs Malcolm X vs The Black Panthers vs JFK

> *I believe in God, who made of one blood all nations that on earth do dwell. I believe that all men, black and brown and white, are brothers, varying through time and opportunity, in form and gift and feature, but differing in no essential particular, and alike in soul and the possibility of infinite development.*
>
> ~W. E. B. Du Bois~

Something that is missing from our ongoing political debate and discourse in Black America today is historical perspective and relevant precedent. Whenever I engage in a political debate, I bring to the fight many past experiences and a historical perspective that my opponent has no idea to which he has no cognitive connection. Therefore, we can seem to be talking past each other because we are not equipped with the same knowledge and fact patterns. When I look at a Democrat, Liberal or so-called Democrat Socialist, I immediately think you are supporting the party and ideology that can rightfully be pegged as the main culprit in the oppression of our Black people for centuries. I am thinking of slavery, 13th, 14th and 15th Amendments, Jim Crow laws, The Ku Klux Klan, Black Codes, Poll Taxes and segregation. These were all perpetuated and championed by the Democrat Party. Democrats look at us Black Conservatives and Trump supporters as aliens, while we look at them as THREE-HEADED ALIENS! How could you support the party that advocated and literally FOUGHT A WAR TO KEEP YOU A SLAVE? How could you support the party that denied you the right of citizenship? How could you support the party that denied you the right to vote? How could you support the party that founded and terrorized our people and White Republicans with the murderous Ku Klux Klan? Yes, White Republicans were lynched also by the Ku Klux Klan. This fact staring in the face of the naked, bold hypocrisy of the left feigning outrage that Donald Trump used the word lynching as a metaphor for how the media and Democrats are unfairly trying to destroy him when, in fact, that term has perfect connotations juxtaposed to what is currently happening to unseat our duly elected president. This is why we have such a steely resolve when defending our position as Trump supporters, Black Conservatives or Republicans.

This brings me to the main theme of this chapter, which may, on its face, throw some for a loop. As I said previously, I bring a historical perspective to my viewpoint on the current state of racial body politics. Donald Trump is being subjugated to the same government tyranny and corruption that many of our Black freedom fighters were victims of in the past in their fight for freedom and equal rights. The Reverend Dr. Martin Luther King Jr. was famously tormented, spied on and lied on. He was secretly recorded by the criminal head of the FBI, J. Edgar Hoover, in compromising sexual situations outside of his marriage. This was deemed very advantageous and a powerful weapon for his opponents with Dr. King being a leader and man of faith and a man of GOD to be used against him. Yes, he was all of these things but also, he was still a MAN with human faults. Luckily for us, a nation of Blacks, Dr. King did not bow to the blackmail and continued his fight for freedom and justice. We are all the richer and thankful for it as Black people, as a nation, and for humanity in general.

POTUS #45 is going through the same types of Marxist opposition, spying and blackmail (think James Comey, the Steele Dossier) as Dr. King. Our United States government law enforcement agencies and international spy agencies have been weaponized against a United States Citizen, his family and anyone tangentially connected to Donald John Trump, Leader of the Free World. Finding yourself in the powerful crosshairs of this behemoth bearing down on you must be quite terrifying. The complete wickedness of the situation arises into your consciousness when you realize you have no recourse because the powers that be that oversee and combats crimes are the same ones illegally coming after you. This is another reason I give POTUS #45 so much credit. He is 70+ years old, a successful billionaire with a supermodel and successful wife and highly intelligent and successful children. He donates his $450k presidential salary to various charities, and his children work for free, with absolutely no salary charged to the government. He has lost billions of dollars on potential deals around the world, yet he subjects himself to be the pinata of the Deep State. He feels so strongly about righting the wrongs of government and their hideous corruption and lost potential on the forgotten people of America he sheds his privileged silver spoon existence to enter the slop-filled pigpen that is American politics. He could be on his own private island like that degenerate Jeffrey Epstein, living the rest of his days with his beautiful family in luxury. The savagery in which he is attacked is also a testament to his willpower, resilience and ability to fight back.

The Deep State has tried to come after Donald J. Trump in many ways and they have been mostly unsuccessful. This is the direct reason you see the unhinged ridiculous zeal that they are going after him with, unrelentingly, until this very day. Their usual tricks and treachery of the political trade have not worked to diminish him in a great way or successfully driven him from office. Since they have been unsuccessful, they try harder and harder and harder. With each successive wave of attack, they become more hateful and more vicious. How dare you stand up to our evil mob mentality and treachery? They must say to themselves. Trump is never cowed, afraid, diminished or seemingly forced to take a proverbial step back. Trump seems to take a step forward and punch the bully in the nose. BAM! Take THAT!!!!! This sends the media and the Dems into a psychotic rage. Never has a Republican stood up to them and fought like hell for his people and followers. For his prize fighter's mentality and toughness in the political arena, Trump has a dedicated following like no other in recent political history. We have become accustomed to Republicans being on the right side of issues and seeing unscrupulous Democrats come and bully them back with lies, corruption and the fake news media. FINALLY, there is someone to stand up for: WE, THE PEOPLE, The Forgotten People.

FBI COINTELPRO – January 22, 1969

Targeting Nation of Islam - FILE: Jan. 22, 1969

Home » FBI COINTELPRO - January 22, 1969

[Note: In this January 22, 1969 previously classified memo, the FBI takes credit for counter intelligence efforts leading to the murder of Malcolm X. The following is a text reproduction of original FBI Document.]

Michael Ameer

DATE: 01/22/1969

TO: DIRECTOR, FBI (100-448006)

FROM: SAC, Chicago (157-2209) (P)

COUNTERINTELLIGENCE PROGRAM

BLACK NATIONALIST - HATE GROUPS

RACIAL INTELLIGENCE

(NATION OF ISLAM)

FBI file information: ReBulet has been thoroughly studied and discussed by the SAC, the Supervisor, and Agents familiar with facets of the NOI (Nation of Islam) which might indicate trends and possible future direction of the organization. The Bureau's concern is most understandable, and suggestions appreciated.

Over the years considerable thought has been given, and action taken with Bureau approval, relating to methods through which the NOI could be discredited in the eyes of the general black populace or through which factionalism among the leadership could be created. Serious consideration has also been given towards developing ways and means of changing NOI philosophy to one whereby the members could be developed into useful citizens and the organization developed into one emphasizing religion - the brotherhood of mankind - and self-improvement. Factional disputes have been developed - the most notable being MALCOLM X LITTLE.

Prominent black personages have publicly and nationally spoken out against the group - U.S.

District Court Judge JAMES BENTON PARSONS being one example. The media of the press has played down the NOI. This appears to be a most effective tool as individuals such as MUHAMMAD assuredly seek any and all publicity be it good or bad; however, if the press is utilized it would appear it should not concentrate on such aspects as the alleged strength of the NOI, immoral activities of the leadership, misuse of funders by these officials, etc. It is the opinion of this office that such exposure is ineffective, possibly creates interest and maybe envy among the lesser educated black man causing them out of curiosity to attend meetings and maybe join, and encourage the opportunist to seek personal gain - physical or monetary - through alignment with the group. At any rate it is felt such publicity in the case of the NOI is not overly effective.

You get a sense here in the preceding paragraphs of this FBI official document from 1969 that they use the press to shape public opinion. Notice how they say that exposing the moral failings of the leadership of the Nation of Islam (NOI) is not that effective because the uneducated negro may be impressed by it or more interested in it. Today is what we call the low-information voter. To have a well-functioning democracy, we must have well-informed voters. We do not have that today in our Black communities. They are told that conservative media are racist. Of course, this is not true, and it deprives them of the necessary knowledge. Still today, the media, the FBI and the Deep State in general have a very low opinion of Blacks and their mental capacity. They play a part in this by feeding lies, falsehoods and omissions. These things along with a terribly failing public school system, have kept many Blacks low information voters. It is hard to digest a multifaceted complex political environment when you are only reading at a secondary school level. Things have not changed in that aspect from now to the 1960's to the 1860's. When you see the amount of lies from the mainstream media today against Donald Trump, you can surmise it is intentional. No way any journalist can make those mistakes or be that dumb. The media are an integral part of the Deep State and just like they worked against Malcolm is the same way they are working against Donald Trump in collusion with our intelligence agencies. When you are abreast of your past, you can use that knowledge to juxtapose that situation with what is happening now and in the present. It gives you a much better perspective.

FEATURES » DECEMBER 4, 2013

How the FBI Conspired to Destroy the Black Panther Party

The assassination of BPP leader Fred Hampton in 1969 was just the beginning.

BY G. FLINT TAYLOR

Share Tweet **Reddit** Email Print

The FBI had, in fact, played a central role in the assassinations, and Hanrahan's initial lies were

only the top layer of what proved to be a massive cover-up.

On Dec. 4, 1969, a select unit of 14 Chicago police officers, under the direction of Cook County State's Attorney Edward Hanrahan, executed a predawn raid on a West Side apartment that left Illinois Black Panther Party (BPP) leaders Fred Hampton and Mark Clark dead, several other young Panthers wounded and seven raid survivors arrested on bogus attempted murder charges. Though Hanrahan and his men claimed there had been a shootout that morning, physical evidence eventually proved that in reality, the Panthers had only fired a single shot in response to approximately 90 from the police.

(http://inthesetimes.com/article/15949/how_the_fbi_conspired_to_destroy_the_black_panther_party)

As we see in the FBI's systematic and brutal takedown of The Black Panther Party, those tactics are still alive today. The FBI and many of its sister agencies are working in concert to subvert and take down Donald Trump, the 45th President of The United States. There is the surveillance and media discrediting that they use against anyone who they deem to be a threat. POTUS #45 was on their radar even before he became President. The alphabet agencies have planted evidence and tried to entrap Donald Trump, his national security adviser and anyone close in his orbit to cash in on that insurance policy Peter Strzok and Lisa Page talked about in their infamous FBI lovers' text messages. Roger Stone, a close friend and supporter of the president, was taken into custody on bogus charges. He was met with a predawn raid of a full SWAT team and amphibious unit in the lake behind his house. The man is 60-plus years old and is being charged with a nonviolent process crime. He would have turned himself in if requested by authorities. They wanted the theater and the ominous look of the predawn raid on camera to give the image of a hardcore criminal being taken off the streets. And low and behold who is there at Stones house at 5 in the morning to catch the festivities, CNN! They said they were not tipped off but just happened to be in the area setting up in front of Roger Stone's house before the complete surprise raid. This folks, is how dumb they think we are.

William C. Sullivan

William C. Sullivan was born in 1912. Sullivan joined the Federal Bureau of Investigation and during the Second World War, he was sent to Spain. He spent several months in Madrid before returning to Washington.

In 1961, Sullivan was appointed assistant director of the FBI's Intelligence Division. Sullivan gradually moved up the hierarchy and eventually became the FBI's third-ranking official behind J. Edgar Hoover, the director, and Clyde A. Tolson. Sullivan was placed in charge of the FBI's Division Five. This involved smearing leaders of left-wing organizations.

When John F. Kennedy was assassinated in Dallas, Sullivan was put in charge of the bureau's in-house investigation. He was expected to work closely with John M. Whitten, who was running the CIA investigation of Lee Harvey Oswald. Whitten and his staff of 30 officers were sent a large amount of information from the FBI. According to Gerald D. McKnight "the FBI deluged his branch with thousands of reports containing bits and fragments of witness testimony that required laborious and time-consuming name checks." Whitten later described most of this FBI material as "weirdo stuff". As a result of this initial investigation, Whitten told Richard Helms that he believed that Oswald had acted alone in the assassination of John F. Kennedy.

However, on 6th December, Nicholas Katzenbach invited John M. Whitten and Birch O'Neal, Angleton's trusted deputy and senior Special Investigative Group (SIG) officer to read Commission Document 1 (CD1), the report that the FBI had written on Lee Harvey Oswald. Whitten now realized that the FBI had been withholding important information on Oswald from him. He also discovered that Richard Helms had not been providing him with all the agency's available files on Oswald. This included Oswald's political activities in the months preceding the assassination.

After talking to Winston Scott, the CIA station chief in Mexico City, Whitten also discovered that Lee Harvey Oswald had been photographed at the Cuban consulate in early October, 1963. Scott had not reported this matter to Whitten, his boss, at the time. Nor had Scott told Whitten that Oswald had also visited the Soviet Embassy in Mexico. In fact, Whitten had not been informed of the existence of Oswald, even though there was a 201-pre-assassination file on him that had been maintained by the Counterintelligence/Special Investigative Group.

Whitten had a meeting with Richard Helms where he argued that Oswald's pro-Castro political activities needed closer examination, especially his attempt to shoot the right-wing General Edwin Walker, his relationship with anti-Castro exiles in New Orleans, and his public support for the pro-Castro Fair Play for Cuba Committee. Whitten added that has he had been denied this information, his initial conclusions on the assassination were "completely irrelevant."

Richard Helms responded by taking Whitten off the case. James Jesus Angleton, chief of the CIA's Counterintelligence Branch, was now put in charge of the investigation. According to Gerald McKnight (Breach of Trust) Angleton "wrested the CIA's in-house investigation away from John Whitten because *he either was convinced or pretended to believe that the purpose of Oswald's trip to Mexico City had been to meet with his KGB handlers to finalize plans to assassinate Kennedy."*

The reports written by Sullivan and Angleton became the basis for the Warren Commission. However, it only emerged in his posthumous published autobiography that Sullivan had doubts about the guilt of Lee Harvey Oswald: "Oswald didn't have a record of being an outstanding marksman and yet he hit the president with two shots while his car was moving slowly down the road. His third shot hit Governor Connally. I went to the book depository from which Oswald fired at the president, and I looked out the window where he was positioned. I've been around guns all my life and

I'm a reasonably good shot, but I must say that that would be quite a task for me. It was, tragically, damn good shooting."

Sullivan was a strong opponent of the leadership of <u>Martin Luther King</u>. In January 1964, Sullivan sent a memo to Hoover: "It should be clear to all of us that King must, at some propitious point in the future, be revealed to the people of this country and to his Negro followers as being what he actually is - a fraud, demagogue and scoundrel. When the true facts concerning his activities are presented, such should be enough, if handled properly, to take him off his pedestal and to reduce him completely in influence."

Sullivan's suggested replacement for King was Samuel Pierce, a conservative lawyer who was later to serve as Secretary of Housing under President Ronald Reagan.

In 1968, Sullivan was the lead investigator into the assassination of Martin Luther King and was involved in the arrest of James Earl Ray. In his autobiography he wrote: "I was convinced that James Earl Ray killed Martin Luther King, but I doubt if he acted alone... Someone, I feel sure, taught Ray how to get a false Canadian passport, how to get out of the country, and how to travel to Europe because he could never have managed it alone. And how did Ray pay for the passport and the airline tickets?" Sullivan believes that Ray was paid to kill King. He quotes Ray's brother as saying: "My brother would never do anything unless he was richly paid."

Sullivan was also involved in the FBI investigation of the assassination of Robert Kennedy. In his autobiography he argued that Sirhan probably acted alone but "we never found out why". He added: "There were so many holes in the case. We never could account for Sirhan's presence in the kitchen of the Ambassador Hotel. Did he know Kennedy would be walking through? Intelligence work is exasperating. You can work on a case for years and still not know the real answers. There are so many unknowns. Investigating Sirhan was a frustrating job, for in the end we were never sure."

Sullivan disagreed with J. Edgar Hoover about the threat to national security posed by the American Communist Party and felt that the FBI was wasting too much money investigating this group.

On 28th August 1971, Sullivan sent Hoover a long letter pointing out their differences. Sullivan also suggested that Hoover should consider retirement. Hoover refused and it was Sullivan who had to leave the organization. Sullivan told the journalist, Robert Novak, soon after he left the FBI: "Someday you will read that I have been killed in an accident, but don't believe it, I've been murdered."

After Hoover's death, Sullivan was brought back to office by Richard Nixon. He was appointed as head of the Office of National Narcotics Intelligence (ONNI). Sullivan supported Nixon's policy of expanding illegal surveillance methods (Huston Plan). Journalists later speculated that Sullivan was Deep Throat, the top-level mole in Nixon's administration who provided some of the important evidence to Bob Woodward and Carl Bernstein in their investigation of Watergate.

William Sullivan was shot dead near his home in Sugar Hill, New Hampshire, on 9th November, 1977. An inquest decided that he had been shot accidentally by fellow hunter, Robert Daniels, who was fined $500 and lost his hunting license for 10 years.

Sullivan had been scheduled to testify before the House Select Committee on Assassinations. Sullivan was one of six top FBI officials who died in a six-month period in 1977. Others who were due to appear before the committee who died included Louis Nicholas, special assistant to J. Edgar Hoover and Hoover's liaison with the Warren Commission; Alan H. Belmont, special assistant to Hoover; James

Cadigan, document expert with access to documents that related to death of John F. Kennedy; J. M. English, former head of FBI Forensic Sciences Laboratory where Oswald's rifle and pistol were tested; Donald Kaylor, FBI fingerprint chemist who examined prints found at the assassination scene.

At the time of his death Sullivan was working on a book with journalist Bill Brown about his experiences with the Federal Bureau of Investigation. *The Bureau: My Thirty Years in Hoover's FBI* was published posthumously in 1979. The book was highly critical of both J. Edgar Hoover and Lyndon B. Johnson.

(https://spartacus-educational.com/JFKsullivan.htm)

As we see here with FBI Agent William C. Sullivan there was much information, disinformation and theory going in the direction of shaping public opinion. The FBI, CIA or Deep State would make their assumption then go about finding their so-called evidence to validate their assumptions. They would also plant, push and manufacture evidence to validate their assumptions. As with all of the aforementioned subjects, MLK, JFK, Malcolm X and The Black Panthers there was a verdict of opinion, then investigations and surveillance enacted to affirm the premeditated verdict.

To have so many in the government, intelligence and security agencies in very sensitive positions next to the President of The United States, John

Fitzgerald Kennedy, one would think how could they have a security lapse of this magnitude? Day after day, we find that Donald John Trump is finding traitors amongst his most trusted cabinet members. Nikki Haley (U.S. Ambassador to The United Nations) under Trump is out with a new book, "With All Due Respect". In her book, Haley asserts that Trumps' Chief of Staff, John Kelly and Secretary of State Rex Tillerson (former Exxon Oil executive) were trying to recruit her to defy Trump to save America. She also stated that she told the president of this attempt by some of his closest cabinet members. It just so happens that as of today, Chief of Staff John Kelly and Secretary of State Rex Tillerson have both been unceremoniously fired by the former "THE APPRENTICE" reality TV star.

As we sit back and connect the dots, we can see a pattern. That word is used many times in this project, **patterns**. The pattern of using or as we say, weaponizing the government apparatus and intelligence agencies to go after your political enemies even though they may also be an unsuspecting part of the government. History repeats itself, especially when most Americans are unaware of the initial infractions. They are weaponizing the government to go after Donald Trump, his family and his supporters just as they have in the past with MLK, Malcolm X, and JFK. RFK and The Black Panthers follow the pattern.

Chapter 4.

"VENOM" THE VICIOUS BLACKLASH AGAINST THE BLACK TRUMP SUPPORTER

> *Why is propaganda so much more successful when it stirs up hatred than when it tries to stir up friendly feeling?*
>
> ~Bertrand Russell~

#CIGARPORN

I can remember when the biggest social pariah was the gay, lesbian and homosexual tag. This was around the 70's, 80's & 90's. Nowadays, it is more widely accepted with million-dollar lobbyists pushing a worldwide LGBTQ sexual agenda. Being transgender and identifying as your sex of choice is almost run of the mill. Now the pariah is to be a conservative, worse than that, a Black Conservative, and worse than that, a Black Trump Supporting Conservative. As we wade into this subject, we can go back to when President Barack Obama held the belief that marriage was between one man and one woman. Then the dollars came rolling in from these lobbies, and whoever you loved was your business, said POTUS #44. In politics, if you follow the money, you will always find a truthful answer.

Since coming out as a conservative many years ago, I have been relentlessly attacked, disparaged, and attempted to be humiliated by venomous ignorant blacks. I say, I was attempted to be humiliated because I had given as much as I had gotten. Recently, over the years, I have not had as many attacks because it is widely known I can debate with political and historical facts for hours and liberals are only armed with recent Democrat talking points and their revisionist history. So, when the conversation gets too deep, they find themselves drowning in the deep water. Knowledge is your best self-defense against these attacks. Many who will attack you with the biggest mouths are the most ignorant of the bunch. Some are lost causes because they do not know what they speak. They only know that THEY HATE TRUMP! Facts, history and knowledge do not matter to these people, for they are bereft of knowledge. TDS, better known as Trump Derangement Syndrome, seems to be a little different from the complete ignoramus. When Trump Derangement Syndrome enters the picture, you have normally calm, levelheaded people who will transform into a hateful, nonsensical, raging lunatic. Just saying the name TRUMP sends them into a tizzy. They have no idea of Trump's accomplishments and have no desire to learn or hear about any of them. Trump could cure cancer, and they would still want him executed immediately. These are just some of the warning triggers for Trump Derangement Syndrome.

As Blacks, we are very sensitive to racism and our history of slavery. The most vitriolic, hateful and racist attacks I have endured have been from the mouths of other Blacks. These Blacks are supposedly, my people! Yet they hold the racist view that you must be a Democrat if you are Black. That, by any definition of the word, is RACIST! This screams racism from the highest mountaintop! The ignorant people who spew this kind of bile think they are correct. They think you would substitute analytical thought, education, knowledge of self and history for skin color. They are so brainwashed that they cannot fathom that a Black person could be highly intelligent and knowledgeable and come to a different political opinion. They are amazed that there is another pattern of thought. This situation is so disappointing because they are so triggered with hate and venom. They won't even take the time to intellectually engage and try to find out why and how you come to your point of view? I have had Europeans and Whites more interested in an opposing point of view than my own people. It was so refreshing to have someone intellectually curious as to how I arrived at my political position, and we engage in real, substantive conversation.

The left and many of our black brothers and sisters are losing the intellectual skill to debate. The left specializes in shutting down debate or trying to find a reason that you should not talk. You are not the right size, shape, color, sexuality or anything else they can find to disqualify you from even commenting on a situation. They spend more time doing this than finding good arguments for their points of view. They have no educated view on conservative thought. They constantly downplay and disparage conservative media and make ridiculous statements regarding it that they cannot back up like Breitbart and Rush Limbaugh for instance. They tell me they are racists, and I say, show me the racist Breitbart article. As a matter of fact, Breitbart puts out tens of thousands of articles a year. Surely, if it is as racist as you say, you can find a handful of racist articles? I am undefeated in my Breitbart challenge.

The same with Rush Limbaugh. At one point, I was binge listening to Rush Limbaugh the whole 3 hour show almost every day, rarely missing a show. Next challenge: tell me what Rush Limbaugh said that you deem racist? Knowing a liberal does not daily, for three hours, listen to Rush is my premise. What they do is listen to someone else, criticize Rush Limbaugh without themselves listening to the whole context. Some liberals are paid to listen to Rush Limbaugh to find one word they can take out of context and attack him and his sponsors and try to get him off the air. Once again, shut down the debate. I don't care what a liberal says or what shows he or she has. I feel I have a better argument.

Let's think back to Kanye West, Steve Harvey, Stacy Dash, Candace Owens and anyone else who has dared to sit and have a conversation with or even a positive thing to say about Trump. They have been savaged in the media, social media and real life. There is a venom saved for Black Conservatives rarely seen in political discourse. Let's take Kanye, for instance. He was vilified, called crazy, stupid, Uncle Tom, coon, showboat and anything negative under the sun. Some radio stations even threatened not to play his music. All of this for a political opinion? Lately, Kanye has jumped the shark and has gone overboard with his antics, and some of those can't be defended.

When they see a slave (Black Conservative) escaping from the Democrat plantation, the House Negroes Spring into action. They chase down the runaway slave and bring him back to his rightful place on the plantation. In today's world, we are not as easily dragged back to the plantation as Steve Harvey. He succumbed to the pressure and is now back on the ole faithful Democrat Plantation. Steve had swift and hard attacks, and it seemed to have blindsided him. He has been sort of apologizing to get back in the good graces of the herd because he is a creature of Hollywood. If you are not a devout liberal, Trump-hating artist, work will be scarce, and ridicule will be plentiful.

In the case of Candace Owens, her quick wit, sharp tongue and wealth of knowledge have Black and white liberals so frustrated and over-emotional trying to demean her. They have gone so far as to call her a white supremacist. They are so shaken and out of character that they stoop to the ridiculous low point of calling an intelligent black woman a white supremacist. This is how far off the deep end they have ventured. Candace Owens is the (former) Director of Communications at Turning Point USA, a conservative advocacy group. She is also the founder of the BLEXIT Movement, which stands for Blacks exiting the Democrat Party. She released a book called BLACKOUT and now has her own show, The Candace Owens Show on The Prager U media platform. This woman is a political dynamo, and the opposition can only attack and try to shut her down. It is amazing what Candace Owens has been able to accomplish in her short time of being a conservative activist. She was even there heading the Young Black Leadership Summit at the Whitehouse with President Trump and hundreds of invited young black conservative activists from all over the United States. Recently, she has turned more anti Trump.

Stacy Dash is a beautiful, talented actress and Trump supporter who has endured probably more venom than most because she has been outwardly conservative for a while. She is routinely bashed and ridiculed by our black brothers and sisters on social media and anywhere they can fit in a dig. She has stood firm amid the barrage of negativity and has been a great spokeswoman for President Trump and conservatism as a political philosophy. The Fox News contributor had also flirted with a run for Congress as a California Republican. She is nevertheless striving and thriving in this venomous political atmosphere.

My hat goes off to any black conservative because it takes tremendous courage and conviction to stand firm on your beliefs. We are today's modern runaway slaves because we know there is a price for speaking the truth to the leftwing mob, media and venomous black liberals. Black conservatives, especially Trump supporting Black conservatives, not only face ridicule, we face physical violence. There have been over 500 documented cases of violent attacks on Trump supporters in the USA. There are countless calls to violence and to attack Trump supporters on social media. This is hideous and uncalled for but done with the blessings of our mainstream media, it will never call out leftwing political violence, like the widespread Antifa cowardice violence. They speak religiously about the violence on January 6th at the U.S. Capital. They lie and say officers were murdered. No officer died on January 6th. Some committed suicide days later and one died of natural causes. They will lie and never get fact-checked by the media on this bold-faced lie. Who died was Ashley Babbitt (Air Force Veteran), who was unarmed and shot point blank in the neck by Officer Michael Byrd (who has since been promoted). Who else died was Roseanne Boyle, who was unarmed and beaten to death. No mention of these Trump supporters' fate when discussing January 6th. It does not fit the narrative and it is an inconvenient truth. This is all left wing politically motivated and gleefully tolerated. This is just another example of the left not being able to compete in the arena of ideas. As of right now, they are burning down Tesla's and Tesla charging stations and keying the cars because they hate Elon Musk for aligning with President Trump and uncovering their corruption.

In a debate normally, when a far-left liberal is losing, he or she will deteriorate into personal insults.

In political rallies and demonstrations, it will often regress into violence. It will almost always come from leftists because they cannot intellectually compete with ideas and arguments. Their weapon of choice is not the mind, facts or a persuasive argument. It is bullying and violence. Very rarely do you see a mob of MAGA hat-wearing thugs smashing windows and beating up defenseless old people. This type of behavior happens unfortunately, much too often in our political discourse and our media tacitly supports it. They will ignore it and when confronted, they will find an excuse for it. This is despicable and shameful.

The left will also plant thugs inside of President Trump rallies to cause violence and then blame it on MAGA. Any violence whatsoever at a President Trump rally will have the media blaming President Trump no matter the originating source of the violence. The left's mantra is THE RESISTANCE! All day, every day, accuse, blame, attack and go after President Trump, his cabinet, his family or his supporters. The venomous hate of the far left knows no bounds.

Chapter 5.

THE KANYE EFFECT

> *If someone hates you for no reason, give that motherf**ker a reason!!!*
>
> ~UNKNOWN~

The mere mention of Kanye West in the Black community sends shock waves, bugged-out eyes, blood pressure bursting stress and hateful outbursts into the atmosphere. After we sift through the excrement of this intolerant nonsense, we can discover some very interesting insights. Blacks are conditioned to hate anyone who is not a Democrat. It's reflexive, it's learned, it's taught by their brainwashing liberal white overseers. Blacks who are pro-Black cannot give their Black brothers and sisters the benefit of the doubt when they find out they are conservative. If you have this visceral reaction to a Black Conservative, then you cannot be pro-Black you are a far-left liberal extremist. If you cannot accept someone of your color with a different political viewpoint, then you are an extremist.

The BIGGEST effect of Kanye is his celebrity. His fan base, his followers, and his influence had a major impact on this political scenario. The White liberal powers knew that if Kanye was left to his own devices to spread his love for Trump and his free-thinking mentality, many of his fans would follow. This would spell doom for the Democrat party. You see, many elections are won on the margins, with the Democrats getting around 95% of the Black vote. We can surmise if the race is close with 95% of the Black vote, the Democrats lose with 80% of the Black vote. Once you see these numbers, you will start to understand how important the Black vote is to the Democratic party. Just a 5- or 10-point swing in the Black vote can be a political EARTHQUAKE.

This political earthquake is why you see the visceral reaction to Black conservatives. With the smallest shift in the Black vote, the Democrat party is brought to its knees. Over the years, the Democrats' identity politics has alienated many of their core voters. They are looking to illegal immigrant votes and any other votes that they can buy with government programs. They've had a war on the white voter, the white male voter, the senior white male voter and obviously your Blue Dog and Reagan-type Democrats. They have allowed Trump to triangulate like Bill Clinton and take their normal standard voters. The Democrat white working-class voters are now voting for Trump.

This is why the reaction to Kanye was monumental. A successful and very influential Black artist stumped for Trump! Kanye's radical outburst was said to double Black male support for Trump from 11% to 22%. A POLITICAL EARTHQUAKE! Trump won 3,080 of 3,141 counties in the 2016 election. 200 counties that went twice for Obama flipped and voted for Trump in 2016. With these numbers, you cannot lose 5-10% of the Black vote. To be competitive in the next election, the

Democrats need to win back some of these voters. They will have a hard time winning back these voters because every day, they are calling Trump voters racists, Nazis, White Supremacists, Cultists, Deplorables, dumb, stupid and anything else negative you can think of.

Kanye has been mercilessly mocked in the media, but he has gone on to head a billion-dollar fashion brand, renewed his support for Trump, became a born again Christian and released a gospel/hip hop album that went #1, "JESUS IS KING"! He is touring the world with his Sunday Service Gospel Concert Series, which seems to be hugely successful. Democrats: HOUSTON, I THINK WE HAVE A PROBLEM! Kanye has proven just as resilient as Trump and just as successful despite the slings and arrows from the so-called WOKE but still asleep community. There are no artists in recent memory who have creatively and courageously put their careers on the line and rolled the dice more than Kanye West, who has beaten the odds and come out on top.

Full disclosure: Kanye West and Jay Z were the last artists from whom I would purchase their CDs with the implementation of digital music media. As fate would have it, Kanye would transform time and time again musically and even politically to have me still interested in what this guy is doing. I must admit this guy is a creative genius, fearless in his pursuit of art. When I witnessed his choir singing in concert, nothing short of amazing. When the music moves you and sounds that good, it's a wrap! He done did it again! But lately Kanye has seemingly crossed the line with his Hitler and Nazi praise. He'd stated previously he was drugged and forcefully institutionalized. That would be the premise of a whole other project.

Chapter 6.

THE NEW ERA BLACK CONSERVATIVE STARS

> *I believe that one defines oneself by reinvention. To not be like your parents. To not be like your friends. To be yourself. To cut yourself out of stone.*
>
> ~Henry Rollins~

There is a new era upon us of fearless, confident, well-read, battle-ready, battle-tested Black Conservative Warriors ready to take the message and the fight to the enemy. No longer are we cowed by misguided public opinion. No longer are we cowed by the venomous attacks of other Blacks. No longer are we cowed by the hateful liberal fake news media that see us as a threat to their power. No longer are we cowed by the limousine liberal elites of the New World Globalist Order. Our numbers and impact on the electorate are growing by leaps and bounds. Knowledge, historical precedent and common sense are our sword and shield. Social media is trying to take us out because of our effectiveness. We spread our message on social media, blogs, face-to-face, and any other medium. In this chapter, I wanted to highlight a few of our Black Conservative Warriors who spread the message and philosophy.

Arguably, one of the most effective and influential new Black Conservatives on the scene is **Candace Owens**. She is deeply hated and vilified by leftists and the mainstream media, which means she is highly successful and effective. That's one thing I noticed on the left. If they bother to waste time, money and resources going after you, you are deemed a threat to them. Suppose you are a conservative and take this as a badge of honor. Candace Owens launched SocialAutopsy.com in 2016, a website she said would expose <u>bullies on the Internet</u> by tracking their digital footprint. This got into a controversy called Gamergate and gamers were going after Candace with doxing and such. At the height of this controversy, Conservatives surprisingly supported Candace. She famously stated she became a conservative overnight, realizing that the liberals were the hateful racist antagonists.

By 2017, she was becoming a well-known conservative pro-Trump political pundit. She was making some amazing YouTube videos titled REDPILL BLACK. These videos criticized the liberal conventional wisdom and promoted Black Conservatism. In November of 2017, she was appointed Director of Urban Engagement by Charlie Kirk of Turning Point USA, a conservative political advocacy group. She would later leave TPUSA amid turmoil and accusations of racism. In April of 2018, Kanye West tweeted, "I LIKE THE WAY CANDACE OWENS THINKS". These mere seven words would set the political mainstream media on fire! The hate for Kanye that reared its ugly head after those few words were savage. Just that small tweet of those seven words unleashed the venomous hate, and the

Black slave catchers sprang into action to track Kanye down and bring him back to his rightful place on the Democrat plantation. Candace and Kanye were the topic of incessant political debate, setting social media on fire. Until this day, surviving the onslaught and criticism both have endured and risen to the top of their professions. Candace has her own show on Prager U and is a Fox News contributor. Candace also founded the Blexit movement, which stands for Blacks Exiting the Democrat party. She is touring America and becoming a huge thorn in the side of liberals who hate to see an intelligent, articulate Black Conservative giving them the business.

"CJ" Pearson (born July 31, 2002) is an American conservative political activist and commentator.

Born in Augusta, Georgia. His political interest deepened at age eight when he started posting blog post in support of local conservative politicians. He embarked on a career as an internet personality when, in early 2015, he uploaded a video to YouTube defending comments made by the former mayor of New York City Rudy Giuliani and criticism of former President Barack Obama, which quickly gained international attention. After the aforementioned event, he began his career as a freelance journalist and has campaigned for several Republican politicians and Bernie Sanders. Pearson describes himself as an "anti-establishment populist" and is described as conservative. He is the executive director of Young Georgians in Government and executive director of Teens for Trump.

"DIAMOND & SILK", aka Lynnette Hardaway and Rochelle Richardson, these African-American sisters are American live stream video bloggers with hundreds of thousands of subscribers, social media personalities, political activists and Fox Nation hosts. They are known for their commentary in support of United States President Donald Trump. They hail from the All-American City of Fayetteville, North Carolina.

"Anthony Brian Logan" is a Youtuber that presents the current events "from the perspective of a young black male conservative and a news/political junkie. He has a very clean, professional presentation with over 345k subscribers. He is a consultant, brand manager, graphic artist, web developer, deep thinker &

natural living expert. ABL is timely and on point with the hot political news of the day.

Chapter 7.

MOVEMENTS AND MEDIA

> "Violence only attacks the body, but it is nonviolence that has the power to influence the soul and reshape it towards a peaceful future."
>
> ~Abhijit Naskar, The Film Testament~

One of the most dynamic movements we have in the political arena today is the **#WalkAwayMovement**. This movement was started by a young, charismatic, gay Hillary Clinton supporter named Brandon Straka. This movement is filled with blacks, whites, Latinos, gays, straight, transgender and everything in between. Here, gather the disgruntled Democrats who are walking away from the Democrat Party. (Brandon has since been arrested at the Trump rally in Washington, D.C., on January 6th, 2021. Although he never entered the capitol building, a "witness" stated that he instructed people to break into the capitol. This is an indictment of Brandon Straka by rumor. NO PROOF!!!!!

The Democrat Party is the self-proclaimed guardian of all black political thought. No other black thought or philosophy is accepted. President Trump is holding massive rallies all over the United States and these rallies are drawing 50,000 or more supporters. The best-kept secret of these rallies is at least 50% of Republicans are attending. That bit of information leaves one to correctly surmise sometimes up to half of these massive crowds can be other than Republican. There have been reports of up to 25% Democrats at Trump rallies. This is massive! Rounding out the crowd are independents, nonaffiliated and first-time voters. The Democrats are so busy trashing Trump and his supporters that they do not realize they are trashing their own. Many Democrats have voted twice for Barack Obama, and this go-round, they thought about giving Trump a chance. These are the people now lumped in with the much-maligned Trump supporters. They are solidifying the #WalkAwayMovement.

The movement has testimonials from former Democrats. This is a very powerful tool. In the testimonials, you get to hear angry, disappointed

Democrats tell their story in their own words. Once you've watched about ten of them, you clearly start to get the picture. Many are disillusioned with the march to the far left fringe of the party. It is a party they no longer recognize. Like Ronald Reagan once said, "I didn't leave the Democrat party, the Democrat party left me."

The #WalkAwayMovement is hosting town halls all over the United States and coalescing online in a formidable social media wave. Brandon Straka is the new toast of the political town. Many who follow the mainstream media are not ready for the big push to upend the normal dynamic, which will be black voters.

BLEXIT! By Candace Amber Owens Farmer. This dynamic, very intelligent, sharp political debater founded the BLEXIT Movement, which stands for Blacks Exiting the Democrat Party. Their mantra is BLEXIT: "WE FREE"! The world is tuning into a new frequency. Across the country, millions of Americans have released themselves from the political orthodoxy. They have unleashed a rebellion of those wishing to disrupt the simulation of fear. This is the intro message on their website www.BLEXIT.com.

The name is a spin-off of BREXIT. The movement of Britain to exit or break away from the European Union finally happened. Populism is finally starting to take root. This is a great mental picture of breaking away or exiting because blacks have been in a unique political space for many decades. We have been owned by the Democrat party like new slaves.

BLEXIT! also uses the visualization of Blacks finally leaving the Democrat Plantation. This growing movement is giving Blacks a platform and support for traditional conservative values and philosophies. They have taken it on the road, around the country and even to Europe to confront the dyed-in-the-wool liberals on their home turf, so to speak. This bold tactic is proving to be fruitful. Just like clockwork, the movement and the founder, Candace Owens are being ruthlessly attacked by the mainstream media and liberals. But this is a badge of honor and of success. They would not waste time and energy attacking you if you were not being effective. This is something I have learned by watching and studying the political landscape. Why do you think they relentlessly attack President Trump?! He is an existential threat to Democrats, liberals and the Republican political establishment. He has also embraced Candace Owens and the BLEXIT! Movement.

BLACK VOICES FOR TRUMP!

Blackvoices.donaldjtrump.com Their website intro states, "Black Voices for Trump will encourage the Black community to re-elect President Donald J. Trump by sharing experiences and successes of everyday people because of the Trump administration. Reelecting the President will ensure greater economic opportunity, safer communities, and better healthcare policies for generations to come (meanwhile, the 2020 election was fraudulently stolen from Donald Trump, more on that later)."

Their advisory board members are a who's who of modern Black Conservatism. They are: Herman Cain (RIP), Co-Chair (has since deceased from COVID-19), Diamond (RIP) & Silk Co-Chair, Pastor Darrell Scott Co-Chair, Robin Armstrong, Deneen Borelli, Reverend C.L. Bryant, Ken Blackwell, Stacy Dash, Paris Dennard, Stephen Gilchrist, Elbert Guillory, Clarence E. Henderson, Keith W. Hodge, Kevin N. Hodge aka The Hodge Twins, Niger Innis, Diante Johnson, Cecilia Johnson, Dr Alveda King (niece of Rev. Dr Martin Luther King Jr.), Sharon Levell, Glenn McCall, Kiyan Michael, Pastor Dean Nelson, Madgie Nicholas, Corrin Rankin, K. Carl Smith, Marie Stroughter, Dr Carol Swain, Dr Linda

Lee Tarver, Stacy Washington and Rep. James White.

When we see this powerful array of fierce, unapologetic Black Conservatism, it shatters the stereotype of Trump supporters. It shatters the stereotype that Trump supporters are all racist old white men, backwood rednecks and white supremacists. The Black Community needs to see more of this. With Black Voices for Trump, there is an aggressive and direct outreach to the Black Community not seen in a century from the Republican Party. I predict this will influence the black electorate in a hugely positive way (my prediction proved to be correct in the presidential election of 2024). Why? Because the outreach is not just empty rhetoric, there is legislation and initiatives to back up the talk.

YOUNG BLACK LEADERSHIP SUMMIT! The Young Black Leadership Summit is an event that welcomes and invites many young black future leaders of the country to The Whitehouse. They are welcomed and addressed by the president himself and inspired to keep fighting for the advancement of issues affecting the black community and the nation at large. Never were there hundreds of Blacks cheering in the Whitehouse for a Republican president. AMAZING!

Opening one summit was BLEXIT founder and Turning Point USA Communications Director Candace Owens. She recounted the story of a 9-year-old Chicago boy, Tyshawn Lee, who left his grandmother's house to play basketball. Tyshawn was approached by an adult black male who befriended him on the basketball court. He lured Tyshawn into an alley, promising to buy him things. Tyshawn was immediately shot and killed at point-blank range in a gang-related slaying. The gang was looking to retaliate against Tyshawn's father and since they could not get the father, they murdered the son. Candace stated that the incident did not garner mainstream media attention because that would put the spotlight and focus on the black-on-black crime that has been ravaging our black communities for decades. Run by Democrat career politicians.

They never confront the problems head-on. They deal with it by blaming Republicans and calling them racists. This tactic is getting old and tired while President Trump is offering an alternative.

We could not talk about The Young Black Leadership Summit without talking about the dynamic **TURNING POINT USA!** TPUSA was founded by a young 18-year-old, Charlie Kirk. It now has 1,000 chapters on college campuses all over the USA.

Not only does TPUSA sponsor the Black Leadership Summit but Turning Point holds other high-level political annual gatherings, including the Young Women's Leadership Summit, the Young Latino Leadership Summit and the Student Action Summit. Turning Point, according to its founder, Charlie Kirk, has established many chapters at college campuses across the country. In a short time, the organization has become quite a force. This is very crucial because college campuses are being overrun with liberal professors producing intolerant liberal students. This is the ideological battlefield. They are brainwashing our youth with this toxic, Marxist hate-filled ideology.

CHAPTER 8.

WELCOMING DIVERSITY

> Isn't it amazing that we are all made in God's image, and yet there is so much diversity among his people
>
> ~Desmond Tutu~

One of the most pleasant experiences I've had transitioning to conservatism all those years ago was and still is the "WELCOME". I have been welcomed with open arms into the conservative community. In my twenty years of proclaiming myself a conservative, I would say I have only encountered two or three that I would label racist. The term the left throws around like frisbees to anyone who disagrees with them on any topic. The talent of the left is they can twist anything into being racist. We can have a conversation about boiling water and at the end of the conversation, SOMEONE will be called a racist.

I have connected with Whites and others and have been able to have fruitful conversations about politics, which are warm and respectful. The most racist reactions I have encountered are from Blacks. Every hateful, mean and racist thing you can endure has been heaped on me by Blacks. Their attacks are vitriolic and condescending. But I have common sense and intelligence, and their ignorance only solidifies my position and proves my point. We say liberals are insufferable and intolerant and then you politically engage, and they prove to be insufferable, intolerant and woefully uninformed and purposefully misinformed.

As a Black man searching for truth and knowledge, you don't have to engage only with like-minded people. You don't mind sharpening your mental blades on some worthy adversary. But sometimes, the conversation can stray so far from common sense that it's senseless to continue.

At this point, I abort the conversation and resort to sarcasm if I choose to continue. I will not waste brain cells on nonsense. Juxtapose this with my conservative experiences and it's night and day. They say conservatives are racists and so on but the conservatives I have met in my travels have been some of the most well-read, intelligent and personable people you could imagine.

The moral condescending high ground that liberals take is laughable. Many subjects that seem relevant to political insiders or just the American people liberals are oblivious to. That lets me know exactly what media outlets they patronize and which ones they don't. When they have no idea what you are talking about, they will attack your sources and say they can't be trusted and you don't know if they are accurate. This is to cover the fact they are flying without radar and don't want to admit they just DON'T KNOW ANYTHING ON THIS SUBJECT!

There are many conservative and populist groups on social media. Visit a few and strike up some conversation and give me some feedback on how it went. Generally, if you are a former or transitioning liberal, you will find conservatives tolerant, welcoming and very hospitable no matter your race, color, religion or background. There is a commonality we have and that's good ole, truth, common sense, fairness and patriotism.

Chapter 9.

WHAT DO YOU HAVE TO LOSE?

> *Do you want to be safe and good, or do you want to take a chance and be great?*
>
> ~Jimmy Johnson~

Everyone was aghast when President Donald John Trump posed this unthinkable question to the Black Community while running for office: "WHAT THE HELL, DO YOU HAVE TO LOSE?" Word on the street is that his political advisors went bonkers, thinking this was not the politically correct way to pose the question. But The Trumpster has uncanny political instincts in which today's verbal blunder becomes tomorrow's brilliant rhetorical flourish. Little did the naysayers know that the blunt, straightforward question would break through and have more Blacks taking a fresh look at President Trump and The Republican Party than at any time in recent memory.

This is a question Black Conservatives have been asking in a different way, "Why do you keep supporting a party that does nothing for the Black Community besides pushing racism?" The state of our inner cities is disastrous. Our children are not reading at acceptable levels. They are not proficient in math, they are not graduating at high percentages, and their college entry test scores are lacking. Our streets are filled with crime, drugs, gang violence, death and murder. These are the main reasons the question resonated with open-minded Blacks. We have all these problems in our communities, but their primary gripe will be "THEY HATE TRUMP."

A poignant question to The Trump Derangement Syndrome sufferers: If you are successful at removing Trump from office, will our public schools educate our kids at acceptable levels? Will the crime drop in our inner cities? Will the gang violence decrease, and we'll have safer communities? Will there be jobs for our people when they finish school? Will drugs and drug trafficking be eradicated? Will someone else help young Blacks released from prison to get jobs? Will our children and their families have school choices? Will HBCU's be aggressively funded? Will financial incentives be given to over 9,000 Opportunity Zones to foster investment in the Black community? These are questions they do not have a reasonable answer for.

The left is not consumed with policies, laws, programs and initiatives that will uplift their people. They are consumed with hating TRUMP! This brings nothing to the advancement of our people. All the previously asked questions are at some level, being addressed by the Trump administration. They are fighting against someone that is fighting for them. They are too consumed with emotional hatred to see that things are being done to address some of the long-simmering problems in our inner-city communities. It seems they would rather their people suffer than for them to flourish under #45!

They seem not to care when we can point to a conservative bringing positive changes to our situation. As I have stated many times, this is the reason Blacks are in the terrible position that we are, under Democrat iron-fisted rule in our urban areas. The goal seems to be to never seek real change. What if all this energy for years going against Trump was put into bettering schools for our kids? Some amazing things could be accomplished. Trump supporters can lay out a laundry list of accomplishments of this administration for the Black Community. What do Trump haters point to as accomplishments from the other side for the people? "NOT MUCH!" That's it and that's sad. A sad situation that leads back to the premise, "WHAT THE HELL DO YOU HAVE TO LOSE?"

Chapter 10.

THIRST FOR BLACK LEADERSHIP

> *"A genuine leader is not a searcher of consensus, but a molder of consensus."*
>
> ~Rev. Dr. Martin Luther King Jr.~

We love our successful rappers. We love our successful basketball players. We love our successful entertainers. What we need more of is successful Black intellectuals. We are missing Frederick Douglas. We are missing Malcolm X. We are missing the next Clarence Thomas. We are missing Thurgood Marshall. We are missing the great Rev. Dr. Martin Luther King Jr. Where can we find the next world-class brain surgeon, as Dr. Ben Carson?

The Black community cannot live on rap and basketball alone. We must start pushing for excellence and not accepting mediocrity from the public school system that shapes our future. We must have leaders bold enough to take on the education system so that system can produce the advanced intellectual leaders we need to sheppard us into the future. Donald Trump has proposed the idea of getting rid of the Department of Education (Ronald Reagan also echoed this sentiment). It may seem radical, but if you look at the precipitous decline in our education system and student test scores, I will fully support that move. No acceptable society should let failure be rewarded. The head of the Department of Education makes $600k and the average bureaucrat there makes $144k. $600k is more than the President of the United States. How can you earn so handsomely presiding over such an abysmal failure? An organization with this track record should be shut down or completely overhauled.

The family unit is being destroyed; the Black family unit is being decimated. We, as a black community, start out in negative territory because the father is the first leader, the first teacher and the first role model. The welfare state started by saying you can get a government subsidy but there must not be a man in the house. This was the beginning of the destruction. We have many things pushed by progressives and liberals that purposefully attack the family unit. We have the proliferation of every sexual orientation besides the healthy heterosexual relationship between a woman and a man. Less heterosexual relationships less traditional family units. Welfare took the male out of the Black home, more single Black mothers, and less traditional family units. More unsupervised young black males, more drugs, more gang violence, more convicted felons and less traditional family units. More planned parenthood in the hood, more Black babies aborted and fewer traditional family units.

As per CNS news: in 2012, there were more Black babies killed by abortion (31,328) in New York City than were born there (24,758), and the Black children killed comprised 42.4% of the total number of abortions in the Big Apple, according to a report by the New York City Department of Health and Mental Hygiene. The report is entitled Summary of Vital Statistics 2012 by the City of New York.

Now, with a massive melting pot as New York City, it is astronomical that Blacks account for almost half of all abortions in the city. A race cannot flourish if it's diminishing. Ask any world leader. The power is in the people. The smaller your numbers, the smaller your influence. The future and future leaders of Black America are being aborted, shot, jailed and marginalized by illegal immigration. This is why there are no substantial changes in the Black community. It is difficult and damn near impossible to nurture strong Black leaders in this climate. But we must try to push for this on every single level possible. The hood stays the same or gets worse and that is a direct result of liberal policies. We need leaders now in a very bad way because we have been brainwashed into following policies and politicians that are detrimental to our race and its existence. This is not a point that can be argued just look at our inner cities. They are devastated. Every major city that has a high crime and poverty rate of 99.9% is run historically by Democrats with ultra-liberal policies. These cities are in a death grip of liberalism. Look at Maxine Waters, Nancy Pelosi and Adam Schiff. Their districts look like third-world countries, and they are running around yelling impeach the president. They are all multimillionaires with dirt-poor constituents for decades and this is how they will continue to run it. Keeping Blacks focused on the ever-present racism will wash their hands of any responsibility for their constituents' living conditions.

We have many new Black Conservative groups that hopefully will breed some great Black leaders. We need action, not virtue signaling and hashtag movements. Our people have settled far too long for symbolism. Whatever symbolism is thrown out there, our kids still can't read at proper levels. Our kids still don't score in math in sufficient numbers. Our kids are still dealing drugs at high levels. Our kids are still joining gangs in record numbers. No leftist symbolism addresses the core problems of our people and that is by design. The leftists' movements are made to consolidate power, not help Blacks. They will have Blacks out there marching to help the elite gain power. Never will you see

Democrats on a national level marching for EDUCATION or STOPPING DRUGS and GANG VIOLENCE.

This makes it impossible to have a real Black leader as a Democrat. If you step off the Democrat plantation, they will cut your foot off. Democrats must toe the line or be severely belittled, chastised, beaten down and marginalized by their own party. Their groupthink comes into play and shrinks every male and capable female of the strong independent voice needed to push for revolutionary changes for their own Black people. They have the go-along-to-get-along mentality. If you piss off the plantation owners, you will no longer have the perks, status and access to wealth that they use to corrupt their ever-ballooning government (Department of

Government Accountability (D.O.G.E.) is attacking this problem). If you ever have the bright idea to go off on your own, they will drag you into that dark dungeon, strap you to a chair and shine that blinding spotlight in your face and give you an offer you can't refuse.

Has Black Culture been reduced to twerking and strip clubs? Has Black Culture been reduced to gangbanging and drug selling? When you think of Black Culture TODAY, what immediately comes to mind? I think if we give an honest answer, we will not come away with many positive images.

Chapter 11.

WHAT HAVE YOU DONE FOR ME LATELY

> *Being busy does not always mean real work. The object of all work is production or accomplishment and to either of these ends there must be forethought, system, planning, intelligence, and honest purpose, as well as perspiration. Seeming to do is not doing.*
>
> ~Thomas A. Edison~

Whenever you pose the question to Blacks, of Blacks supporting a Republican or a conservative, they always come up with the same question. What have conservatives done for Blacks? But the more important question is: What have Democrats done for Blacks? This is the most important question of all. The Democrats run the ghettos and inner cities and have an almost monolithic, slavish dedication of Blacks to the Democrat party. So, to the people who give their support, vote and authority to one party, what are they doing for you? "NOTHING!"

We look back on what the Democrat party has done for Blacks and it's to keep them on the hamster wheel. The hamster wheel of racism. Tell Blacks that Republicans are racist. That was the culmination of their outreach and pitch to the Black community. The administrator of Populist Wire, a populist political media site that I am a contributor to posted a telling comic. The comic was of a father handing a cookie to a child, then the father asks. "What's the magic word to get what you want?" The child answered, RACIST!!! It's funny as hell because it is true. Racism and identity politics are the mother's milk of the progression of the left. Without racism or the perceived threat of racism, the Democrat Party would cease to exist.

The left has racism, identity politics and FREE SHIT as its platform! They push the notion that the government is supposed to take care of you and all your needs from cradle to grave. This disincentivizes hard work and achievement. This has given rise to the deadbeat politician Bernie Sanders. A self-described Democratic Socialist. But a real socialist and communist sympathizer. Sanders had never had a real job until he was elected mayor of Burlington at 39 years of age. He has been a career politician for almost 40 years, and this is the unaccomplished loser that the Democrats far, far out of their left wing want to lead the free world. The "tax and spend" policies of Sanders and his ilk have done nothing but ravage Black communities. They always promise pie-in-the-sky bullshit that never pans out to its original intentions. You don't have to look left or right. Just look at your hood and tell me if your current leaders are delivering results for you, your family and your community.

Well, my friends, I have an answer for you this time when you ask what Republicans have done for Blacks.

1. The First Step Act (Criminal Justice Reform).

The Formerly Incarcerated Reenter Society Transformed Safely Transitioning Every Person Act or First Step Act reforms the federal prison system of the United States of America and seeks to reduce recidivism. An initial version of bill H.R. 5682 was sponsored by Rep. Douglas Collins [R-GA-9] (Introduced 05/07/2018) and passed the House of Representatives (360–59) on May 22, 2018; a revised bill passed the U.S. Senate (on a bipartisan 87–12 vote) on December 18, 2018. The House approved the bill with Senate revisions on December 20, 2018 (358–36). The act was signed by President Donald Trump on December 21, 2018, before the end of the 115th Congress. The act, among many provisions, retroactively applies the Fair Sentencing Act, allows for employees to store their firearms securely at federal prisons, restricts the use of restraints on pregnant women, expands compassionate release for terminally ill patients, places prisoners closer to family in some cases, authorizes new markets for Federal Prison Industries, mandates de-escalation training for correctional officers and employees, and improves feminine hygiene in prison.

The legislation increases the number of good conduct time credits that prisoners receive from 47 days per year to 54 days. Due to a legislative drafting error, this change is not being applied retroactively.[1]

Donald Trump designated April 2019 as First Step Act Month at a 1 April 2019 ceremony.

This is something that the Democrats have been "TALKING" about for many years and they have done absolutely nothing on this monumental issue. Donald Trump has taken many similar issues and turned them into his own issues. This is a problem that has been plaguing the Black community for decades, yet it takes a supposed racist to go to Washington, D.C. and get it done!

The First Step Act also will work against recidivism. There are job placement programs, training and many US Corporations have pledged to hire the formerly incarcerated so they have an alternative to the criminal activities that lead them to prison in the first place. This is a blessing that provides hope. Hope and opportunity in the Black community are as necessary as the air we breathe. More than 90% of the people who benefit from this program are Black! Ivanka Trump and Jared Kushner have been instrumental in bringing this to the Presidents attention and letting him know there is broad support from both parties to get it done.

Question: Why would a racist keep doing things to benefit Blacks?

President Trump and his administration are proactive in successfully transitioning Americans who are reentering society from prison to jobs. The Department of Labor recently released $84.4 million in grants to community groups, states and localities to advance programs that will help reduce crime and fill open jobs.

2. **National Minority Enterprise Development Week**, also known as **National MED Week**, is a special week in the month of October, observed in the United States, to recognize and celebrate the achievements and contributions of the minority business enterprise community. In 2017, the administration officials attended the

event, which was held at Cobo Arena in Detroit, with over 5,000 people in attendance.

President Ronald Reagan first recognized National MED Week in 1983. Each year, every President of the United States officially recognizes National MED Week through a Presidential Proclamation. The week is formally celebrated each year by the Minority Business Development Agency, a U.S. government agency housed within the U.S. Department of Commerce.

President Donald Trump became the first President of the United States to formally recognize minority-owned businesses in the Oval Office during National MED Week, when he welcomed winners of the National MED Week Awards on October 24, 2017. On October 20, 2017, President

Trump issued a proclamation to officially designate October 22 through October 28, 2017 as National Minority Enterprise Development Week.

The **Minority Business Development Agency** holds an awards ceremony each year during National MED Week to recognize the contributions of minority-owned businesses in a variety of industry categories. These awards include:

- Minority Business Enterprise of the Year
- Minority Construction Firm of the Year
- Minority Export Firm of the Year
- Minority Manufacturing Firm of the Year
- Minority Energy Firm of the Year
- Minority Technology Firm of the Year

- Minority Health Products and Services Firm of the Year

- Minority Marketing and Communications Firm of the Year

- Minority Professional Services Firm of the Year

- Abe Venable Legacy Award for Lifetime Achievement

- Access to Capital Award

- Advocate of the Year Award

- Distinguished Supplier Diversity Award

- Ronald H. Brown Leadership Award

Trump stated in his speech that the awardees were honored by the fact that minority-owned companies employ more than 8 million people and generate more than a trillion dollars in economic output. He talked of the tremendous potential of the inner cities and said that he is always looking for ways to bring in more economic opportunities. The goal is to lift barriers so minority-owned businesses can prosper. Thirty million Americans who own small businesses will get a 40% cut in their marginal tax rate. This is the lowest rate in over 80 years since 1931. This along with deregulation will spur great economic growth and bring opportunity to more sections of the inner cities.

3. **President Trump signs Executive Order to permanently fund Historically Black Colleges:**

The federal HBCU initiative office was moved back into the White House, a move that leaders had requested under President Obama.

EXECUTIVE ORDERS

Presidential Executive Order on The White House Initiative to Promote Excellence and Innovation at Historically Black Colleges and Universities

EDUCATION

Issued on: February 28, 2017

By the authority vested in me as President by the Constitution and the laws of the United States of America, and in order to advance opportunities in higher education, it is hereby ordered as follows:

Section 1. Policy. Historically black colleges and universities (HBCUs) have made, and continue to make, extraordinary contributions to the general welfare and prosperity of our country. Established by visionary leaders, America's HBCUs have, for more than 150 years, produced many of our Nation's leaders in business, government, academia, and the military and have helped create a black middle class. The Nation's more than 100 HBCUs are located in 20 States, the District of Columbia, and the U.S. Virgin Islands and serve more than 300,000 undergraduates, graduate and professional students. These institutions are important engines of economic growth and public service, and they are proven ladders of intergenerational advancement.

A White House Initiative on HBCUs would advance America's full human potential, foster more and better opportunities in higher education, strengthen the capacity of HBCUs to provide the highest-quality education, provide equitable opportunities for HBCUs to participate in Federal programs, and increase the number of college-educated Americans who feel empowered and able to advance the common good at home and abroad.

Section 2. White House Initiative on HBCUs.

(a) Establishment. There is established The White House Initiative on Historically Black Colleges and Universities (Initiative), housed in the Executive Office of the President and led by an Executive Director designated by the President.

(b) Mission and Functions. The Initiative shall work with agencies, private-sector employers, educational associations, philanthropic organizations, and other partners to increase the capacity of HBCUs to provide the highest-quality education to an increasing number of students. The Initiative shall have two primary missions:

    (i) increasing the private-sector role, including the role of private foundations, in:

        (A) strengthening HBCUs through enhanced institutional planning and development, fiscal stability, and financial management; and

(B) upgrading institutional infrastructure, including the use of technology, to ensure the long-term viability of these institutions; and

(C) enhancing HBCUs' capabilities to serve our Nation's young adults by:

    a. strengthening HBCUs' ability to equitably participate in Federal programs and exploring new ways of improving the relationship between the Federal Government and HBCUs;

    b. fostering private-sector initiatives and public-private partnerships while promoting specific areas and centers of academic research and program-based excellence throughout HBCUs;

c. improving the availability, dissemination, and quality of information concerning HBCUs in the public policy sphere;

d. sharing administrative and programmatic best practices within the HBCU community;

e. partnering with elementary and secondary education stakeholders to build a "cradle-to-college" pipeline; and

f. convening an annual White House Summit on HBCUs to address, among other topics, matters related to the Initiative's missions and functions.

(c) Federal Agency Plans.

(i) The Secretary of Education (Secretary), in consultation with the Executive Director, shall identify those agencies that regularly interact with HBCUs.

(ii) Each agency identified by the Secretary under subsection (c)(i) of this section shall prepare an annual plan (Agency Plan) describing its efforts to strengthen the capacity of HBCUs to participate in applicable Federal programs and initiatives. Where appropriate, each Agency Plan shall address, among other things, the agency's proposed efforts to:

(A) establish how the agency intends to increase the capacity of HBCUs to compete effectively for grants, contracts, or cooperative agreements;

(B) identify Federal programs and initiatives where HBCUs are not well represented, and improve HBCUs' participation in those programs and initiatives; and

(C) encourage public-sector, private-sector, and community involvement in improving the overall capacity of HBCUs.

(iii) The head of each agency identified in subsection (c)(i) of this section shall submit its Agency Plan to the Secretary and the Executive Director no later than 90 days after being so identified, and submit an updated Agency Plan annually thereafter.

(iv) To help fulfill the objectives of the Agency Plans, the head of each agency identified by the Secretary may provide, as appropriate, technical assistance and information to the Executive Director to enhance communication with HBCUs concerning the agency's program activities and the preparation of applications or proposals for grants, contracts, or cooperative agreements.

(v) Each agency identified by the Secretary shall appoint a senior official to report directly to the agency head on that agency's progress under this order, and to serve as liaison to the Initiative.

(d) Interagency Working Group. There is established an Interagency Working Group, which shall be chaired by the Executive Director and shall consist of one representative from each agency identified by the Secretary pursuant to subsection (c)(i) of this section, to help advance and coordinate the work required by this order.

Section 3. President's Board of Advisors on HBCUs.

(a) Establishment. There is established in the Department of Education the President's Board of Advisors on Historically Black Colleges and Universities (Board). The Board shall consist of not more than 25 members appointed by the President. The Board shall include the Secretary, the Executive Director, representatives of a variety of sectors — such as philanthropy, education, business, finance, entrepreneurship, innovation, and private foundations — and sitting HBCU presidents. The President shall designate one member of the Board to serve as its Chair, who shall help direct the Board's work in coordination with the Secretary and in consultation with the Executive Director. The Chair shall also consult with the Executive Director regarding the time and location of the Board's meetings, which shall take place at least once every 6 months.

(b) Mission and Functions. The Board shall advise the President, through the Initiative, on all matters pertaining to strengthening the educational capacity of HBCUs. In particular, the Board shall advise the President in the following areas:

(i) improving the identity, visibility, distinctive capabilities, and overall competitiveness of HBCUs;

(ii) engaging the philanthropic, business, government, military, homeland-security, and education communities in a national dialogue regarding new HBCU programs and initiatives;

(iii) improving the ability of HBCUs to remain fiscally secure institutions that can assist the Nation in achieving its educational goals and in advancing the interests of all Americans;

(iv) elevating the public awareness of, and fostering appreciation of, HBCUs; and

(v) encouraging public-private investments in HBCUs.

(c) Administration. The Department of Education shall provide funding and administrative support for the Board, consistent with applicable law and subject to the availability of appropriations. Members of the Board shall serve without compensation, but shall be reimbursed for travel expenses, including per diem in lieu of subsistence, as authorized by law. Insofar as the Federal Advisory Committee Act, as amended (5 U.S.C. App.), may apply to the Board, any functions of the President under that Act, except for those of reporting to the Congress, shall be performed by the Chair, in accordance with guidelines issued by the Administrator of General Services.

(d) Report. The Board shall report annually to the President on the Board's progress in carrying out its duties under this section.

Section 4. Revocation of Executive Order. Executive Order 13532 of February 26, 2010 (Promoting Excellence, Innovation, and Sustainability at Historically Black Colleges and Universities), as amended, is revoked.

Sec. 5. General Provisions. (a) For the purposes of this order, "historically black colleges and universities" shall mean those institutions listed in 34 C.F.R. 608.2.

(b) (b) This order shall apply to executive departments and agencies designated by the Secretary. Those departments and agencies shall provide timely reports and such information as is required to effectively carry out the objectives of this order.

(c) The heads of executive departments and agencies shall assist and provide information to the Board, consistent with applicable law, as may be necessary to carry out the functions of the Board. Each executive department and agency shall bear its own expenses of participating in the Initiative.

(d) Nothing in this order shall be construed to impair or otherwise affect:

(i) the authority granted by law to an executive department or agency, or the head thereof; or

(ii) the functions of the Director of the Office of Management and Budget relating to budgetary, administrative, or legislative proposals.

(e) This order shall be implemented consistent with applicable law and subject to the availability of appropriations.

(f) This order is not intended to, and does not, create any right or benefit, substantive or procedural, enforceable at law or in equity by any party against the United States, its departments, agencies, or entities, its officers, employees, or agents, or any other person.

DONALD J. TRUMP

THE WHITE HOUSE,

February 28, 2017.

4. OPPORTUNITY ZONES

President Donald J. Trump Is Lifting Up American Communities That Have Been Left Behind

ECONOMY & JOBS

Issued on: **April 17, 2019**

We're providing massive tax incentives for private investment in these areas to create jobs and opportunities where they are needed the most.

President Donald J. Trump

ENCOURAGING INVESTMENT: Opportunity Zones will spur private-sector investment to

revitalize hurting communities and unleash their economic potential.

- In 2017, President Trump signed the Tax Cuts and Jobs Act, which established Opportunity Zones to incentivize long-term investments in low-income communities across the country.

- These incentives offer capital gains tax relief to investors for new investment in designated Opportunity Zones.

- Opportunity Zones are anticipated to spur $100 billion in private capital investment.

- Incentivizing investment in low-income communities fosters economic revitalization and job creation and promotes sustainable economic growth across the Nation.

LIFTING UP COMMUNITIES: Opportunity Zones help drive economic growth and lift up communities that have been left behind.

- Opportunity Zones are a powerful vehicle for bringing economic growth and job creation to the American communities that need them the most.

    o On average, the median family income in an Opportunity Zone is 37 percent below the State median.

    o The average poverty rate in an Opportunity Zone is more than 32 percent, compared with a rate of 17 percent for the average United States census tract.

- More than 8,760 communities in all 50 States, the District of Columbia, and 5 Territories have been designated as Opportunity Zones.

  o Nearly 35 million Americans live in communities designated as Opportunity Zones.

CREATING OPPORTUNITY FOR ALL: President Donald J. Trump is encouraging investment to create opportunity in distressed communities.

- In 2018, President Trump signed an Executive Order establishing the White

House Opportunity and Revitalization Council.

- o The Council is chaired by the Secretary of Housing and Urban Development, Ben Carson, and is comprised of 16 Federal agencies.

- The Council is engaging all levels of government to identify best practices and assist leaders, investors, and entrepreneurs in utilizing the Opportunity Zone incentive to revitalize low-income communities.

- The Council is improving revitalization efforts by streamlining, coordinating, and targeting existing Federal programs to economically distressed areas, including Opportunity Zones.

- o Lack of coordination and targeting has led to cumbersome applications, program waste, and ineffective benefits.

- The Council will consider legislative proposals and undertake regulatory reform to remove barriers to revitalization efforts.

- The Council will present the President with a number of reports identifying and recommending ways to encourage investment in economically distressed communities.

This opinion piece from Jill Homan of The Washington Examiner opines on the success of the program and it miraculously being able to bring Democrats and Republicans together.

OPINION

Bipartisan success of Opportunity Zones gives Trump an edge

by Jill Homan

| February 27, 2020 12:00 A

(EXCERPT)

"The Opportunity Zone tax incentive was part of the Tax Cut and Jobs Act, signed into law by Trump in December 2017. Opportunity Zones give economically distressed communities a second chance by offering investors tax benefits for providing qualifying capital to these areas. There are over 8,700 low or moderate-income census tracts designated as Opportunity Zones throughout all 50 states, Washington, D.C., and five U.S. territories with 35 million people residing in them.

Since its inception, this program has received bipartisan support due to its creative approach to assisting communities that need it most.

District of Columbia Mayor Muriel Bowser, a Democrat, embraced Opportunity Zones by nominating 25 designated spots as possible growth areas for investors. K Street tech firm, <u>Enlightened,</u> recently teamed up with a development firm to invest in an Opportunity Zone in Anacostia. Enlightened CEO Antwayne Ford sees this as a win-win for both his company and local workers. "My attitude is if I have a job in technology, I'm willing to train folks to do it. They are ready to come right here in their own neighborhood to work that should shift the paradigm."

She is not the first Democratic mayor to embrace Opportunity Zones for her city. Across the country, mayors from both parties have sung the policy's praises. For instance, Braddock, Pennsylvania, Mayor Chardae Jones's designation of 23 Opportunity Zones attracted a vertical farming company called Fifth Season, which opened a headquarters in Braddock with the promise of employing at least 60 people. Braddock's Council President Tina Doose shared, "There will be local folks from [ZIP code] 15104 that will be employed at this facility. And to hear that commitment does my heart well."

5. Strengthening 401k Portability for small minority owned and employed businesses

FACT SHEETS

President Donald J. Trump is Strengthening Retirement Security for American Workers

ECONOMY & JOBS

Issued on: August 31, 2018

It's time to take care of our people, to rebuild our nation, and to fight for our great American workers.

President Donald J. Trump

EXPANDING ACCESS TO RETIREMENT PLANS: President Donald J. Trump signed an executive order to expand access to workplace retirement savings plans for American workers.

- President Trump is directing the Departments of Labor and the Treasury to consider issuing regulations and guidance that would make it easier for businesses to offer retirement plans.

    o The Departments will consider changes to make it easier for businesses to join together to offer Association Retirement Plans (ARPs), also known as Multiple Employer Plans.

- ARPs reduce the cost of offering retirement plans for businesses that join together by expanding the number of workers who participate.

    o Currently, complying with the requirements has made it difficult for small businesses to band together to offer ARPs.

- Workers at small businesses often have less access to workplace retirement plans compared to workers at larger businesses.
    - Eighty-nine percent of workers at establishments with 500 or more employees are offered a workplace retirement plan.
    - In contrast, only 53 percent at establishments with fewer than 100 workers are offered a workplace retirement plan.

REDUCING COSTS FOR SMALL BUSINESSES: High costs prevent many small businesses from offering workplace retirement plans, weakening the retirement security of their employees.

- High costs are holding back small businesses from offering workplace retirement plans, as they do not benefit from the economies of scale that larger businesses enjoy.

    o Businesses that offer workplace retirement plans pay administrative and overhead costs that may be difficult for small businesses to afford.

- Small businesses say high costs are discouraging them from offering workplace retirement plans, according to a Pew survey.

    o Seventy-one percent of small and medium sized businesses that do not offer workplace retirement plans reported that high costs deterred them from doing so.

- o Thirty-seven percent of small and medium sized businesses cited high costs as their main reason for not offering a plan.

- The executive order directs the Departments of Labor and the Treasury to consider ways to improve notice requirements to reduce paperwork and administrative burdens.

STRENGTHENING WORKERS' FINANCIAL FUTURES: Making changes to certain retirement plan rules will help workers better prepare for their financial futures.

- The Department of the Treasury is to review the rules on required minimum distributions from retirement plans to see if retirees could keep more money in 401(k)s and Individual Retirement Accounts for longer.

- o This could allow retirees to spread retirement savings over a longer period of time.

- Polling shows that nearly half of all Americans are concerned they will not have enough money to live on during retirement.

- Too many American workers, including one-third of those in the private-sector, have no access to workplace retirement plans, burdening them with concerns about their financial futures.

BET Founder Bob Johnson praised President Trump at a White House event for a program that will benefit low-income black and Hispanic Americans.

6. Lowest Black Unemployment Rate in History

Pastor Darrell Scott (Black Voices for Trump) excerpt from article in the Delaware Gazette Nov., 14th, 2019

"Since Donald Trump's inauguration, the U.S. economy has created a whopping 1,017,000 new jobs for African Americans, including many right here in Ohio. Today, the national black unemployment rate is at an all-time low of 5.5 percent. Unemployment for black women is even lower, at just 4.4 percent. More importantly, the overall black-white employment gap is smaller than it has ever been. It is great to see so many African American men and women back in the workforce — more than ever before, in fact."

Historic U.S. Job Market Continues as African-American Unemployment Rate Hits New Low

November 1, 2019

Council of Economic Advisers

Today, the Bureau of Labor Statistics (BLS) released its monthly Employment Situation Report, which shows continued employment growth and a low unemployment rate in October. Job gains at this point in the business cycle are particularly noteworthy, considering that the United States is in the midst of the longest economic expansion in its history.

BLS's establishment survey shows total nonfarm payroll employment increased by 128,000 jobs last month, far exceeding the median market expectation of 85,000. Including a substantial upward revision of 95,000 total jobs for the months of August and September and controlling for the estimated 60,000 decrease because of the recently resolved General Motors (GM) strike and the 20,000 decrease from temporary U.S. Census workers finishing their work, this report highlights the creation of over 300,000 new jobs.

Since the President's 2016 election, the economy has added over 6.7 million jobs—more than the combined populations of Wyoming, Vermont,

Alaska, North Dakota, South Dakota, Delaware, Rhode Island, and Montana in 2018. Additionally, this total is 4.8 million more jobs than the Congressional Budget Office projected would have been created in its final forecast before the 2016 election.

BLS's separate household survey finds that the U.S. unemployment rate increased slightly from its 50-year low of 3.5 percent in September to 3.6 percent in October, marking the 20th consecutive month at or below 4 percent unemployment. Most notably, the unemployment rate for African Americans reached a new series low of 5.4 percent, falling 2.6 percentage points since President Trump's election.

The labor force participation rate, which includes workers and those looking for work, increased to 63.3 percent in October—0.6 percentage point above the rate in November 2016. The labor force participation rate for prime-age adults (ages 25-54), which largely avoids the demographic effects of the aging population, increased by 0.2 percentage points in October to 82.8 percent—1.4 percentage points above its rate in November 2016. Small changes in labor force participation can have major effects on the economy: Because of this increase, 2.1 million more prime-age adults were in the labor force in October compared to if the participation rate remained at November 2016 levels.

Steady job growth, accompanied by 15 months of 3 percent or higher average year-over-year hourly wage increases, benefits Americans across the country, as 24 States achieved or matched their lowest-ever unemployment rates during the Trump Administration. As of September 2019 (the latest available State unemployment data), 35 States had unemployment rates below 4 percent, compared to 14 States when President Trump was elected.

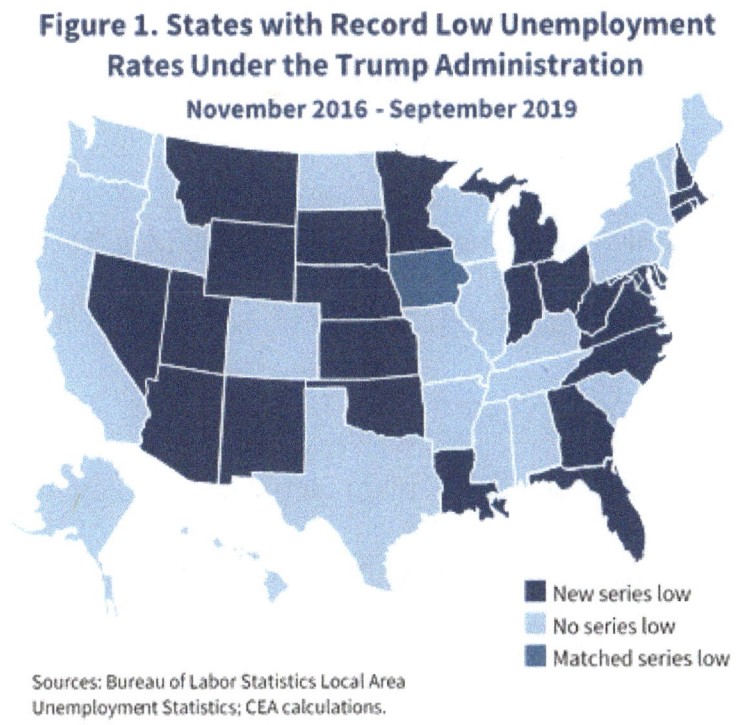

Figure 1. States with Record Low Unemployment Rates Under the Trump Administration
November 2016 - September 2019

Sources: Bureau of Labor Statistics Local Area Unemployment Statistics; CEA calculations.

While today's release shows that manufacturing employment fell by 36,000 during October, this decline is fully explained by the 40-day strike at GM. The Department of Labor's (DOL) monthly strike report showed 46,000 GM workers were on strike during the October payroll survey. Workers on strike do not collect a paycheck, so they do not count as employed. Additionally, the negative effects of the strike reverberated throughout the economy, including lowering employment at GM suppliers, leading to an estimated 60,000 total employment decrease in October. The strike's resolution portends manufacturing employment bouncing back in November, adding to the gains seen over the Trump Administration.

Even with the strike lowering October's manufacturing numbers, nearly 500,000 manufacturing jobs have been created since the 2016 election. This growth is why the National Association of Manufacturers quarterly outlook survey reached its highest recorded confidence level during the Trump Administration. Comparatively, 20,000 manufacturing jobs were lost in the 12 months prior to the 2016 election.

Evidence of a robust job market is also supported by private sector surveys. The Conference Board measures employment optimism as the share of respondents claiming that jobs are plentiful minus those who think they are tough to obtain. Using this measure, employment optimism for October (35.1 percent) was much higher than it was in November 2016 (6.6 percent).

Figure 2. Labor Market Differential, 2001–19
Percentage points

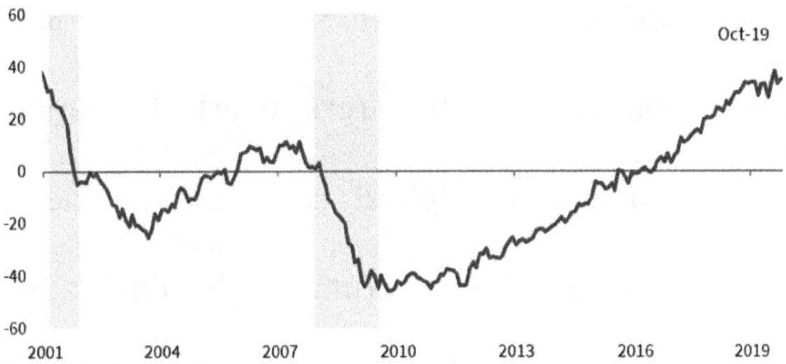

Source: The Conference Board.
Note: The labor market differential is the difference between the percentage of consumers who think jobs are plentiful and the percentage who believe that jobs are currently hard to get. Shading denotes a recession.

With consistent job gains this far into the longest economic recovery in U.S. history, the October employment data make it clear that the American labor market remains strong. States across the country continue setting record-low unemployment rates, showing how Federal policies that support economic growth benefit local communities. American workers see these benefits as today's labor market offers them opportunities to negotiate raises and advance their careers.

7. SCHOOL CHOICE

"The American Federation for Children, the nation's voice for educational choice, and Beck Research, a Democratic polling firm, released their fifth annual National School Choice Poll today. The survey of 1,200 likely November 2020 voters showed that 67% of voters support school choice, an increase of 4 percentage points compared to the 2018 National School Choice Poll."

American Federation for Children

Tommy Schultz, January 17th, 2019.

America wants School Choice; Blacks want School Choice but Democrats do not want School

Choice. Why are Democrats bucking the system on school choice? Simple because they are in the pocket of the teacher's union, so they do not give a damn about the education and learning of our children in this woefully inept and underperforming public school system. How and why do Blacks support the very people who say it is better to keep your kids in a failing school system? Every parent wants the best for their children. Why not a better school system?

Project Baltimore analyzed 2017 state testing data and found one-third of High Schools in Baltimore, last year, had zero students proficient in math.

Why is this story not one of the top stories in America? To be earnest and frank, the media, the

Dems and the powers that be do not give a sh*t about educating Black people. This is a crisis for a people and a nation if large segments of our society are not educated. For our type of government, we have to have a fully involved, engaged and informed electorate. This is hard to do without it starting in the schools.

Making America Great Again

Education

President Donald J. Trump Achievements

President Trump's proposed budgets have made school choice a priority.

- **The President's FY2018 Budget Request included $1 billion in funding to Furthering Options of Children to Unlock Success**

Grants for public school choice and $250 million to promote private school choice through the Education Innovation and Research Program.

- In his FY2019 budget President Trump proposed a $5 billion federal tax credit on donations that fund scholarships to private and vocational schools, apprenticeships programs and other educational opportunities.

The Trump Administration successfully implemented the Every Student Succeeds Act (ESSA) to empower states with the flexibility they need to educate their students.

- 35 states and the District of Columbia have had their ESSA plans approved and the Department of Education is reviewing the plans for the remaining states.

- The Department of Education is urging states to embrace the opportunity provided by ESSA to end top-down mandates from Washington, D.C.

The Trump Administration implemented the year-round distribution of Pell grants, instead of limiting these grants to the spring and fall semesters.

- Low-income students will now have access to these funds over summer and winter breaks, so they can earn their degrees faster with fewer loans.

The Trump Administration reformed the student loan servicing process to improve customer experience and lower costs.

The Trump Administration has reformed The Free Application for Federal Student Aid to make the program more accessible to students.

The Trump Administration brought in financial experts to modernize the way FSA offers and services student loans.

The Department of Education provided $359.8 million in federal assistance to 20 states and the U.S. Virgin Islands to assist with the cost of educating students displaced by Hurricane Harvey, Irma, Maria, or the 2017 California wildfires.

8. SHRINKING INCOME INEQUALITY

- American workers of all backgrounds are thriving under President Trump.

  o The unemployment rates for African Americans, Hispanic Americans, Asian Americans, veterans, individuals with disabilities, and those without a high school diploma have all reached record lows under President Trump.

- The booming economy is putting more money in Americans' pockets.

  o Wages are growing at their fastest rate in a decade, with year-over-year wage gains exceeding 3 percent for the first time since 2009.

- November 2019 marked the 16th consecutive month that wages rose at an annual rate of at or over 3 percent.

- Median household income surpassed $63,000 in 2018 – the highest level on record.

• President Trump's policies are helping forgotten Americans across the country prosper, driving down income inequality.

- Wages are rising fastest for low-income workers.

- Middle-class and low-income workers are enjoying faster wage growth than high-earners.

- When measured as the share of income earned by the top 20 percent, income inequality fell in 2018 by the largest amount in over a decade.

• Americans are being lifted out of poverty as a result of today's booming economy.

- Since President Trump took office, over 2.4 million Americans have been lifted out of poverty.

- Poverty rates for African Americans and Hispanic Americans have reached record lows.

- Since President Trump's election, nearly 7 million Americans have been lifted off of food stamps.

- Americans are coming off of the sidelines and back into the workforce.
  - The prime age labor force has grown by 2.1 million under President Trump.
  - In the third quarter of 2019, 73.7 percent of workers entering employment came from out of the labor force rather than from unemployment, the highest share since the series began in 1990.
- President Trump's pro-growth policies are helping businesses of all sizes thrive like never before.
  - Small business optimism broke a 35 year old record in 2018 and remains historically high.

- o The DOW, S&P 500, and NASDAQ have all repeatedly notched record highs under President Trump.

- President Trump is following through on his promise to revitalize American manufacturing, with more than a half million manufacturing jobs added since the election.

- President Trump has prioritized workforce development to ensure American workers are prepared to fill high quality jobs.

  - o The President has worked to expand apprenticeship programs, helping Americans gain hands-on training and experience with no student debt.

- Since President Trump took office, over 660,000 apprentices have been hired across the country.

- President Trump established the National Council for the American Worker, tasked with developing a workforce strategy for the jobs of the future.

- Over 370 companies have signed the President's "Pledge to America's Workers," pledging to provide more than 14.4 million employment and training opportunities.

- President Trump signed an Executive Order prioritizing Cyber Workforce Development to ensure that we have the most skilled cyber workforce of the 21st century.

- President Trump signed the Tax Cuts & Jobs Act in 2017 – the largest tax reform package in history.

  o More than 6 million American workers received wage increases, bonuses, and increased benefits thanks to the tax cuts.

  o $1 trillion has poured back into the country from overseas since the President's tax cuts.

- President Trump is revitalizing distressed communities through Opportunity Zones, which encourage investment and growth in underserved communities.

- More than 8,760 communities in all 50 States, the District of Columbia, and 5 Territories have been designated as Opportunity Zones.

- The White House Opportunity and Revitalization Council has taken more than 175 actions to encourage investment and promote growth within Opportunity Zones.

- The White House Opportunity and Revitalization Council is engaging all levels of government to identify best practices and assist leaders, investors, and entrepreneurs in using the Opportunity Zone incentive to revitalize low-income communities.

9. YOUNG BLACK LEADERSHIP SUMMIT

The Young Black Leadership Summit, the brainchild of former communications director of TPUSA, (Turning Point USA) Candace Owens. TPUSA founded by young Charlie Kirk with 1400 clubs all over the USA in high schools and colleges, were welcomed into The Whitehouse by President Trump. He welcomed them in October of 2019 for the second time, over 300 young Black conservative leaders and Trump supporters from all over the United States descended upon Washington, D.C.

This was a time to network, and for the young Black conservatives to actually meet and talk with the president, his staff, get encouragement and build upon their leadership skills. This was a 3-day summit, with 17 speakers including POTUS #45. The summit was sponsored by Liberty University and The Heritage Foundation.

The young leaders were in support of the President because of things like The First Step Act, criminal justice reform, his pro-Christianity stance, immigration, opportunity zones and low Black unemployment. Their support was evident with the raucous welcome they gave the president on his entrance into the room and up to the podium.

The president was very gracious to give his time and kind words to these young African American leaders of the future. This will be a moment in their lives that will never be forgotten. Many times, the media pushback against a Republican president as it pertains to the Black community is stifling. Not many Republicans will even attempt to address

Black audiences, but Trump has been unabashedly courting the Black vote with some success. Some polling has shown great strides in the Black community, but it remains to be seen how it will turn out with the votes on election day.

10. H.R. 267 Martin Luther King Jr. National Historical Park

President Donald J. Trump Signs H.R. 267 into Law

Issued on: January 9, 2018

On Monday, January 8, 2018, the President signed into law:

H.R. 267, the "Martin Luther King, Jr. National Historical Park Act," which redesignates the Martin Luther King, Junior, National Historic

Site in the State of Georgia as the Martin Luther King, Jr. National Historical Park.

1. National Diversity Coalition for Trump

NDC Mission

National Diversity Coalition for Trump strongly supports President Donald Trump and his administration. Our group represents the voices of our communities. President Trump's vision for the United States includes creating opportunities for men, women, and children of all racial, economic, and educational backgrounds. We support the President and his solutions that address economic disparities, foster job creation, support small businesses, preserve faith & family principles, and strengthen communities with conservative action. We will recruit, mobilize, and educate citizens to help us support President Trump and his administration throughout his presidency.

2. PARDONING JACK JOHNSON (posthumously)

Statement from the Press Secretary Regarding the Pardon of John Arthur "Jack" Johnson

<u>LAW & JUSTICE</u>

Issued on: May 24, 2018

Today, President Donald J. Trump issued an Executive Grant of Clemency (Full Pardon) posthumously to John Arthur "Jack" Johnson, the first African American Heavyweight Champion of the World, for a Mann Act conviction that occurred during a period of racial tension more than a century ago. Johnson served 10 months in Federal prison for what many view as a racially motivated injustice.

Born in 1878 in Galveston, Texas, to former slaves, Johnson overcame difficult circumstances to reach the heights of the boxing world and inspired generations with his tenacity and independent spirit.

Congress has supported numerous resolutions calling for Johnson's pardon. These resolutions enjoyed widespread bipartisan support, including from the Congressional Black Caucus. One of these resolutions passed Congress as recently as 2015.

In light of these facts and in recognition of his historic athletic achievements and contributions to society, the President believes Jack Johnson is worthy of a posthumous pardon. President Trump is taking this unusual step to "right a wrong" that occurred in our history and honor the legacy of a champion.

CHAPTER 12.

THE KARDASHIAN EFFECT

> *You should never be defined by what you do, by the things you have; you've got to define yourself by who you are and who you impact and how you impact people. And that's the thing I try to get across to my players.*
>
> ~Tony Dungy~

Kardashian and the 45th President of The United States, Donald John Trump at first glance seem like polar opposites. Little did anyone know that Kim Kardashian was following the plight of Alice Marie Johnson. Alice Marie Johnson is a 63 year old African American grandmother who was doing life for a first-offense non-violent drug crime of passing some information. This gross injustice motivated the megastar socialite Kardashian to contact Jared Kushner and Ivanka Trump. This led to a lobbying of President Trump to take a look at this case. This case of course started with a gross miscarriage of justice in the sentencing of Ms. Johnson. She spent 21 years of a life sentence in The Federal Correctional Facility in Dublin, California. She was sentenced in 1997 for her part in a Memphis, Tennessee drug operation. Ms. Johnson inevitably became a model inmate. Alice Marie Johnson was later transferred to a federal hospital prison in Texas (Federal Medical Center, Carswell). There, she became a certified hospice worker. Subsequently, she was transferred to a federal prison in Aliceville,

Alabama to be closer to her family. During her sentence, she had also become an ordained minister and counseled other inmates. Ms. Johnson was working on her appeal for clemency in hopes that it would be granted by President Obama at the time. President Obama eventually granted clemency to 1,927 people, but unfortunately, Alice Marie Johnson was not one of those people. In working for her clemency, Johnson was allowed to make interviews with preapproved online media platforms. One of those interviews got the attention of Kim Kardashian and the rest they say, is history. Alice Marie Johnson has been to the White House multiple times and has met the president and even has spoken at events lauding the successes of The First Step Act (Criminal Justice Reform). This is what

I call the Kardashian Effect, meaning anyone could make a difference and have an effect on a person's life in Trump's Whitehouse. Kanye West has even been there to meet the president and have his ear on issues. Jim Brown was a legendary pro football player, along with many other Black athletes and Black leaders.

Back in 2018, when the controversy was really hot over the NFL players kneeling during the National Anthem at games, Trump issued a challenge or olive branch, whichever you may think is appropriate. Trump publicly asked NFL players whom he should pardon. He asked if you know of someone who was unfairly treated, to send me their names, and he would look into their case and see if a full pardon or commutation would be warranted.

No NFL players accepted the offer. This is why the chapter Thirst for Black Leadership is so important. It seems Blacks would much more accept the symbolism of taking a knee or raising a fist than the tangible physical act of getting one of their own released from an unfair prison sentence. This is one of the biggest points of this endeavor. We as a people would rather pose and impress friends as SJW's (social justice warriors) than get into the trenches as MLK or Malcolm X and fight for change. It really saddened me that LeBron James, an icon in the Black community said he would not sit down with President Trump and talk. On the other hand, he seemed to support the outright racist regime of China, The CCP and The Chinese Communist Party that openly discriminates against Black Americans and Africans. But they do finance the NBA with very big bucks.

Too many of our Black leaders stand against injustice but never accomplish any change except swelling their own bank accounts. LeBron James, Colin Kaepernick, Jesse Jackson, Al Sharpton and Maxine Waters are all millionaires who spend more time building a bullshit narrative against the president than making sure their constituents and followers are progressing and living their best lives. What if Martin Luther King Jr. would not sit down with presidents and influential leaders? Where would we be today if our civil rights trailblazers of the past would adopt this and never talk to anyone in power who could improve the situation of our people? President Trump has one of the most progressive open-door policies I have seen in a Whitehouse administration. Why don't we use it? Kim Kardashian said she was not a huge supporter of the president, but she had the common sense to understand that this man had the power to right a terrible injustice. We are cutting off our nose to spite our face, leave the nose on, it's beautiful!

CHAPTER 13.

LOUIS FARRAKHAN EYE TO EYE

> "The eye through which I see God is the same eye through which God sees me; my eye and God's eye are one eye, one seeing, one knowing, one love."
>
> ~Meister Eckart~

Louis Farrakhan has been a very powerful voice in the Black community for many decades. Minister Farrakhan has come up through the ranks of the Nation of Islam (NOI) along with Malcolm X, boldly leading and inspiring generations of young Blacks. He had come along and was present during the clash of Malcolm X and The Honorable Elijah Muhammad.

Also, during this time, there was a connection and mentoring of the ultimate boxing legend Cassius Marcellus Clay, who later famously converted to Islam under the name Muhammad Ali and became affectionately known to the boxing world simply as "THE GREATEST". Minister Farrakhan was also disparagingly nicknamed Calypso Louis by the world's most famous radio talk show host, conservative pundit Rush Limbaugh (Farrakhan was formerly a calypso musician) and was many things to many people. He was and probably still is one of the most dynamic and charismatic firebrand public speakers of our time.

Now, in the days of political correctness, his often outright blatant racism and antisemitism are not as palatable or needed as they once were. I say

NEEDED in the sense of our coming out of the civil rights movement when Blacks were denied their basic civil rights and an argument for Black Power could have been made and justified. He is not as welcomed nowadays in mainstream America. His Jew-Bashing has been oft putting for many. The Minister has been called on many times to mediate street beefs within the hip-hop and gang communities. He helped defuse those confrontations before they turned violent. Minister Farrakhan found himself in a unique position, I cannot remember any other individual in recent history, with this credibility, except maybe Nelson Mandela. He is respected amongst the street thug and gang culture, the religious world as a representative and leader of The Nation of Islam, and a world leader seen as a respected voice of the Black experience in America conversing with leaders on the world stage. Love him or hate him, never has there been a man who could walk with influence in as many different worlds.

I was an avid follower of Minister Farrakhan and was reading much literature on Islam when I found myself deployed to Iraq in the first Gulf War as a Combat Medic. I was seriously contemplating converting to Islam but felt I was not ready to follow all the strict guidelines at that point in my life, while still fundamentally believing in Traditional Christian values. I was spiritual and not really any kind of religious zealot. I was still a sinner, drinking, partying, running the streets, an aspiring rapper based in Germany, where I still reside to this day. I surmised that if I could not go all in 100%, then I would not do it at all. But I would listen to tapes of Farrakhan and some of my friends and I were mesmerized by this captivating speaker. At this point, I was more into Black History, civil rights and our post-slavery struggle, which later led me to politics. Still intrigued with Islam, I gave up pork and soda, which ended up being a good health reason more than religious, although over the years, I have back slid on the soda but no pork on the fork, except for an occasional pepperoni pizza (the guilty pleasure).

I started to part ways with the minister when, in Germany, I married a German woman and had two very beautiful, loving children from that relationship. The kids were bright, intelligent, well-mannered, handsome, and some of the top athletes in the country. Their mother gave them much of that good upbringing. Today, one is a lawyer and the other has earned a master's degree. So how can I look at a beautiful half-white family and say you are the DEVIL??!! This antisemitism and constant racist theme separated me from Minister Farrakhan because I had contradictory life experiences from my time in the U.S., the Army and traveling the world as a musician. My experiences formed my outlook on people being more alike than we are unalike. From my studying of politics, I felt MONEY and POWER were the basic fuel of evil. Politicians and leaders use race as a weapon, but that weapon helps them get to the ultimate prize of money and power. They say power corrupts and absolute power corrupts absolutely. A perfect example is the Democrats posing as the friends of Blacks to get their vote, promising them everything then giving them nothing but a few government handouts. Their weapon of choice is The Republicans are racists, and your kind (Blacks) belongs over here with us Democrats. We will take care of you.

> *"The Democrats are playing you for a political CHUMP and if you vote for them, you are not only a CHUMP, you are a traitor to your race!" The Ballot or the Bullet*
>
> *~Malcolm X*

This quote from Malcolm is profound in the sense that it resonates so many years later. The only difference is Blacks do not feel that they are a traitor to their race. They are blindly voting against their best interests and the White Liberals will get them to do this every few years come election time. Also paraphrasing something Malcolm X said, the White Liberal will always pose as the friend of the Negro, a wolf in sheep's clothing. Beware of the White liberal who will put himself in charge of a Negro organization. A Negro organization by name should be led by a Negro. We see today that many Black groups are backed, controlled and funded by Whites or others just using them as a means to a political end. This quote by Malcolm X puts it more succinctly.

> "The white liberals who have been posing as our friends, have failed us. The white liberal is the worst enemy to America, and the worst enemy to the Black man, White liberals have perfected the art of selling themselves to the Black man as our "friend" to get our sympathy, our allegiance and our minds. The white liberal attempts to use us politically against white conservatives, so that anything the Black man does is never for his own good, never for his own advancement, never for his own progress, he is only a pawn in the hands of the white liberal."
>
> ~Malcolm X

When I contemplate those words, the first thing that comes to mind is the border wall. Immigrants come in lower wages and drain public program funds from the Blacks who need them. The white liberal will have Blacks protesting and marching supporting "ILLEGAL" immigration and criminal protecting sanctuary cities, which said earlier drains the resources that could be better, more efficiently dispersed rightfully for the deserving legal Black and minority citizens. We have such a high crime rate in our inner-city communities. Why would we protect criminals, illegal ones at that and let them back on our streets? Looking through this lens is THE BLACK TRUMP SUPPORTER! It is very profound that something said so long ago could be as relevant today, but amazingly it is!

This brings me to the recent statements in a radio interview with minister Louis Farrakhan where we once again can see EYE TO EYE. The interviewer stated that people argue that the so-called racism of the Trump administration is more in our faces than hidden. (Radio WGCI 107.5 Chicago)

Farrakhan: Well, that wasn't the intent of this administration to do a lot for us. But the nature of this administration is good for us. Because now you know, sometimes you think you are where you are not, so Trump is letting you know where you really stand. And because of Trumps' way, he is an anomaly. There has never been a president quite like Mr. Trump. But there's something that he's doing. I am going to come out in a few weeks and talk about it, but Trump is destroying every enemy that has been an enemy of our rise. Who's the enemy of our rise? Is it the Department of Justice where we get none? Is it Congress where you make a law that favors us then they turn around and destroy it? Is it the media that has destroyed every Black leader that stood up for us? Calling us out of our name. Martin

Luther King suffered it, Malcolm suffered it Duboise suffered it, Marcus Garvey suffered it, so he's attacking the media, calling it fake news. Well, I don't think everything is fake, but I know very well that we have been the victims of some fake news. He's beating up the FBI (hand claps) go at it, baby!!!! Because they've been beating the hell out of us ever since J. Edgar Hoover and the COINTEL program of the U.S. government, so go ahead, Mr. Trump!

This interview very pointedly sums up this whole chapter. Donald Trump is fighting and being attacked by the same DEEP STATE that destroyed our Black leaders and the civil rights movement. This is what frustrates me so much with the Black community. They are supporting the same apparatus that destroyed our civil rights leaders and our fight for freedom. The white liberals have fed them so much racism on top of racism and history revisionism they are blinded by anything with a racist tag, real or perceived! This blindness and irrational rage are affectionately called TRUMP DERANGEMENT SYNDROME! They do not have a rational thought pattern of juxtaposing history with today.

What they are doing to the Trump Administration is corrupt. They are turning every part of the government into a weapon to set up, frame and take down a duly elected President of the United States. Many cheer this on because they deem the administration racist (although they can point to no real racist policies). Corruption is a cancer; you cannot turn it off and on like a light switch. Sooner or later that DEEP STATE may turn once again, against you and your interests. When that happens, you have no legs to stand on because CORRUPTION was ok when it was against your PERCEIVED enemy. Now, once it hits close to home, many will scream injustice and cry foul, but remember, it was all good just a week ago, when it was used in your favor. This is the moment you realize it's about POWER, not RACE!

Barack Hussein Obama was the first Black/ or half-black POTUS. He was a liberal doing exactly what the DEEP STATE wanted so he was used for the progress of their agenda items like illegal immigration and managing the decline of America, its assets and its economy. They used a Black man to get black people to support radical positions that were detrimental to the progress and growth of their own people. So once again here is the point. It's not about race, it's about power. They elevated a Black man to the highest office in the world because it suited their plans for a New World Globalist Order and POWER!

CHAPTER 14.

THE BLACK BOOK

> *A small body of determined spirits fired by an unquenchable faith in their mission can alter the course of history.*
>
> ~Mahatma Gandhi~

The Black Book is a compilation of names of Black conservatives that would behoove you to research and listen to and explore their history and direction in no order. The Black Book comes from all different professions, backgrounds and walks of life. Some of these people you may know of, or you may not, but the point is to give you as much information as possible on their political outlook. This is your homework assignment. THE BLACK BOOK:

Allen Bernard West is an American political commentator, retired U.S. Army lieutenant colonel, author, and former member of the U.S. House of Representatives. A member of the Republican Party, West represented Florida's 22nd congressional district in the House from 2011 to 2013.

Alveda King, Alveda Celeste King is an American activist, author, and former state representative for the 28th District in the Georgia House of Representatives. She is the niece of civil rights leader Martin Luther King Jr., the daughter of civil rights activist A. D. King, and his wife, Naomi Barber King.

Anthony Brian Logan is a black conservative political commentator and writer from Virginia Beach, Virginia, by way of Charleston, West Virginia, who now resides in East Tennessee. He grew up in a single-parent household but always had the love and support of not only both parents but also that of a large extended family. While being raised in a socially conservative household, Anthony's views were very politically liberal until well into adulthood when his "red pill moment" happened. At that point, he became more of a conservative person.

Armstrong Williams is an American political commentator, entrepreneur, author, and talk show host. Williams writes a nationally syndicated conservative newspaper column, has hosted a daily radio show, and hosts a nationally syndicated television program called The Armstrong Williams Show.

Brandon Tatum is a former Tucson Police Officer and served as the Director of Urban Outreach at Turning Point USA. He is the Founder and CEO of The Officer Tatum, LLC. He is an unapologetic conservative firebrand.

Burgess Owens' path to Congress is a story of resilience and a staunch commitment to conservative principles. A former NFL player, his life took a dramatic turn towards public service, driven by a deep-seated belief in individual liberty and economic opportunity. He emerged as a powerful voice, particularly on issues of race and social policy, challenging prevailing narratives and advocating for self-reliance. His election to the U.S.

House of Representatives from Utah's 4th congressional district marked a significant moment, bringing a unique perspective to the Republican caucus. Owens, a Black conservative, speaks passionately about his experiences and his vision for America, often drawing on his own journey to illustrate the power of hard work and personal responsibility. His narrative resonates with those who feel marginalized by mainstream political discourse, and he has become a prominent figure in the conservative movement.

Byron Donalds, a rising figure in the Republican Party, carries a story that defies easy categorization. Hailing from Florida's 19th district, his journey to the halls of Congress is one of a self-described "Trump-supporting, gun owning, liberty-loving, pro life, politically incorrect Black man." His roots lie in finance, a world of numbers and pragmatism, before he transitioned to the political arena, serving in the Florida House of Representatives.

Candace Owens, Candace Amber Owens-Farmer is an American conservative commentator and political activist. She is known for her pro-Trump activism and her criticism of Black Lives Matter and of the Democratic Party. She worked for the conservative advocacy group Turning Point USA between 2017 and 2019. Founder of The BLEXIT Movement.

Carol Miller Swain is an American conservative television analyst and former professor of political science and law at Vanderbilt University. She is the author and editor of several books. Her scholarly work has been cited by two associate justices of the Supreme Court of the United States.

Chicago Flips Red (Danielle Carter-Walters) The organizers of "Chicago Flips Red" weren't content with mere rhetoric. They were determined to translate their convictions into political action, to mobilize Black voters and reshape the city's political landscape. Meetings were held, community leaders spoke out, and a new narrative began to emerge. The goal was clear: to challenge the established order, to flip the city from blue to red, and to send a message that the traditional political allegiances were no longer set in stone. The movement was a direct challenge to the Democratic power structure and a clear embrace of Trump's policies.

The winds of change were blowing through Chicago, a city long considered a Democratic stronghold. A movement, stark and resolute, was taking root within the Black community: "Chicago Flips Red." It wasn't a gentle nudge; it was a decisive break from decades of political tradition. Frustration with the Democratic Party, once a reliable ally, had reached a boiling point.

This wasn't a movement of quiet dissent. It was a vocal embrace of Republican ideology, a full-throated endorsement of Donald Trump. The issue of illegal immigration became a rallying cry. Trump's hard-line stance resonated with many who felt their communities were being overlooked their concerns dismissed.

CJ Pearson, Coreco Ja'Quan Pearson is an American conservative political activist and commentator. Born in Augusta, Georgia, Pearson was raised in Grovetown. His political interest deepened at age eight, when he started posting blog post in support of local conservative politicians

Clarence Thomas is a conservative American judge, lawyer, and government official who currently serves as an Associate Justice of the Supreme Court of the United States. He is currently the most senior associate justice in the court, following the retirement of Anthony Kennedy.

Condolezza Rice, Condoleezza "Condi" Rice is an American political scientist, diplomat, civil servant, and professor. She served as the 66th United States Secretary of State, the second person to hold that office in the administration of President George W. Bush.

Darrell C. Scott is an American pastor and a member of President Donald Trump's executive transition team. He is a co-founder of the New Spirit Revival Center in Cleveland Heights, Ohio. He is a co-founder, along with Michael D. Cohen, and a board member of the National Diversity Coalition for Trump.

Diamond & Silk, Lynnette "Diamond" Hardaway R.I.P. (November 25, 1971 – January 8, 2023) and Rochelle "Silk" Richardson, known as Diamond and Silk, are American livestream video bloggers, social media personalities, political activists and Fox Nation hosts. They are known for their commentary in support of United States President Donald Trump.

Dr. Ben Carson, Benjamin Solomon Carson Sr. is an American politician, public servant, author and retired neurosurgeon serving as the 17th United States Secretary of Housing and Urban Development since 2017. The first and only pediatric neurosurgeon to successfully separate conjoined twins.

Edward William Brooke III was an American Republican politician. In 1966, he became the first African American popularly elected to the United States Senate. He represented Massachusetts in the Senate from 1967 to 1979.

Erika Natalie Louise Harold, Harold was born in Urbana, Illinois. Her ethnicity includes Greek,

German and English on her father's side; and on her mother's side, she is both Native American and African American. She graduated from the University of Illinois, Phi Beta Kappa with a B.A. in political science and was a Chancellor's Scholar. In 2007, she received her J.D. from Harvard Law School, where she won best brief in the Harvard Ames Moot Court semi-final and final rounds of competition. She has worked in Chicago, Illinois, as an associate attorney at Sidley Austin LLP and at Burke, Warren, MacKay & Serritella. She currently works for Meyer Capel law firm in Champaign, Illinois.

Herman Cain (RIP) was an American politician, business executive, syndicated columnist, and Tea Party activist. Cain grew up in Georgia and graduated from Morehouse College with a bachelor's degree in mathematics.

His arrival in the U.S. House in 2021 marked a distinct voice within the conservative movement. He stands as a staunch advocate for his principles, a voice that cuts through the noise of Washington's political theater. His presence challenged conventional narratives, offering a perspective that resonated with a growing segment of the American electorate. He was a Black conservative congressman who was not afraid to say what he believed.

James Golden, under the pseudonym **"Bo Snerdley,"** serves as call screener, producer, and engineer for the syndicated Rush Limbaugh radio talk show. Since 2001, he has been a

Producer/Executive for Premiere Networks, the largest radio syndication company in the United States.

Janice Rogers Brown is a former United States Circuit Judge of the United States Court of Appeals for the District of Columbia Circuit. She was an Associate Justice of the California Supreme Court from May 2, 1996, until her appointment to the D.C. Circuit. She retired from the federal bench on August 31, 2017.

Jim Brown (RIP) was an athlete, actor and activist. He was a legendary African American football player, actor, and civil rights advocate.

Ken Blackwell, John Kenneth Blackwell is an American politician, author, and conservative activist who served as the mayor of Cincinnati, Ohio, the Ohio State Treasurer, and the Ohio Secretary of State. He was the Republican candidate for governor of Ohio in 2006, the first African American major party candidate for governor of Ohio

Larry Elder, Laurence Allen "Larry" Elder is an American libertarian attorney, author, and radio program host. He is one of the most dynamic conservative speakers and debaters on the scene today.

Lynne Martine Patton was designated in June 2017 by President Donald Trump to head Region II of the United States Department of Housing and Urban Development, which oversees New York and New Jersey.

Thomas Sowell is an American economist and social theorist who is currently a senior fellow at the

Hoover Institution at Stanford University. Sowell was born in North Carolina but grew up in Harlem, New York. He dropped out of Stuyvesant High School and served in the United States Marine Corps during the Korean War. Brilliant common sense comes in no better package.

Vernon Jones, Vernon Jones is an American Democratic politician from the U.S. state of Georgia. Jones was chief executive officer of Dekalb County, Georgia, from 2001 until 2009 and in the Georgia House of Representatives from 1993 to 2001. Vernon Jones is one of the first Black Democrats to publicly denounce his party, cross party lines and support President Trump.

Walter Edward Williams is an American economist, commentator, and academic. He is the

John M. Olin Distinguished Professor of Economics at George Mason University, as well as a syndicated columnist and author known for his classical liberal and libertarian conservative views.

Wardell Anthony "Ward" Connerly is an American political activist, businessman, and former University of California Regent. He is also the founder and the chairman of the American Civil Rights Institute, a national non-profit organization in opposition to racial and gender preferences.

Zora Neale Hurston was an American author, anthropologist, and filmmaker. She portrayed racial struggles in the early 1900s American South and published research on hoodoo. The most popular of her four novels is Their Eyes Were Watching God, published in 1937.

Chapter 15:

Trump/Vance 2024 (The Greatest Comeback in Political History)

In the rearview mirror of political history, there will never be another comeback quite like 2024 for the 45th and 47th President of the United States, Donald John Trump. President Trump is uniquely qualified to withstand the slings and arrows thrown by the Deep State.

Cigar Lounge Trump International, Dubai, UAE

Reflecting on this election, my conversations with Ms Lindy Li provided a fascinating glimpse into the world of big-money politics. Her experience from being the youngest congressional candidate to a key fundraiser for Kamala Harris, revealed the inner workings of a campaign and the impact of its financial stewardship. The implosion of the Harris campaign, as she described it, highlighted a disconnect between the campaign's actions and the expectations of its donors, a sentiment shared by many who contributed their hard-earned money.

Donald Trump, in stark contrast, has consistently faced opponents with vastly superior financial resources. Hillary Clinton and Kamala Harris, between them, commanded staggering sums, exceeding a billion dollars in campaign funds. Yet, despite this financial advantage, their campaigns faltered. Harris suffered a decisive defeat, losing all swing states and the popular vote, a significant shift in the political landscape.

The magic, as always, is in the message. And from my perspective as a Black conservative, the Trump/Vance 2024 victory signifies more than just a political comeback; it represents a realignment of the American political landscape. This election was a referendum on the very soul of the nation, a battle between entrenched political elites and the forgotten men and women of America.

Trump's message resonated with those who felt ignored and disenfranchised by the established political order. His focus on economic nationalism, border security, and a return to traditional values struck a chord with working-class Americans, including many in the Black community who saw their own economic and social concerns reflected in his platform.

The Trump/Vance ticket, a blend of populist energy and intellectual rigor, presented a compelling alternative to the status quo. Vance's sharp intellect and understanding of the challenges facing middle America complemented Trump's instinctive connection with the electorate. Together, they formed a formidable team capable of challenging the prevailing narratives and mobilizing a diverse coalition of voters.

This election wasn't just about personalities; it was about principles. It was about a rejection of identity politics and a reaffirmation of the American ideal of equality under the law. It was about prioritizing the needs of everyday Americans over the interests of special interest groups and political insiders.

The Trump/Vance victory was a testament to the enduring power of the American spirit, a reminder that even in the face of overwhelming odds, the will of the people can prevail. This comeback will be etched in the annals of history, a defining moment that reshaped the political landscape and reaffirmed the enduring promise of the American dream.

The 2024 election wasn't just a political contest; it was a seismic shift, a resounding declaration from the American people. Donald Trump, facing a relentless barrage of legal challenges, challenges his supporters, and increasingly, many others, decried as politically motivated "lawfare", stood as a defiant figure against what was perceived as a deeply entrenched political establishment. The mainstream media, once holding the mantle of trusted information, now found its pronouncements met with widespread skepticism, its credibility fractured. The trust in traditional media outlets and the Democratic party had plummeted, fueled by accusations of pervasive bias and a growing sense of detachment from the concerns of everyday Americans.

Trump's "drain the swamp" rhetoric, initially dismissed as political grandstanding, resonated far beyond his core base. Millions of Americans, regardless of party affiliation, felt alienated by the bureaucratic machinery of Washington, perceiving a "deep state" acting against the nation's interests. The legal battles played out in the glaring spotlight of media coverage were seen by many as evidence of this entrenched power's attempts to silence a voice that dared to challenge the status quo.

The media, instead of acting as a neutral arbiter, was increasingly viewed as an active participant in the conflict. News reports were dissected, analyzed, and dismissed as biased by a growing segment of the population, who sought alternative sources of information. Social media, once a tool for connection, became a battleground of competing narratives, amplifying the distrust of traditional media.

Crucially, Trump's message transcended his established base. It tapped into a widespread sentiment of disillusionment and a yearning for change. He spoke directly to the anxieties and frustrations of those who felt overlooked and bypassed by the forces of globalization and political correctness. His rallies, filled with a diverse coalition of Americans, became powerful demonstrations of his connection with the electorate. This connection translated into a significant victory at the ballot box. Trump won the popular vote, a testament to the broad appeal of his message, not just among his base but across the American landscape.

The 2024 election was a watershed moment, a decisive rejection of the established order and a reaffirmation of the power of the people. It wasn't simply a political victory; it was a cultural and societal realignment. The deep state, the media, and the entrenched political establishment had underestimated the depth of the American people's desire for change. They had underestimated the power of a message that resonated with millions, a message that propelled Donald Trump back into the White House, with the undeniable mandate of the popular vote.

Happy New Year 2024 Frankfurt, Germany

The Black Trump Supporter

All White Birthday Party Vibes

Chapter 16.

TRUMPS' RACIST TENDENCIES

> "The soul is the same in all living creatures, although the body of each is different."
>
> ~ Hippocrates.

The relationship between Donald Trump and Michael Jackson was a notable one, and it spanned a period where Jackson faced significant public scrutiny. Donald Trump and Michael Jackson were acquainted, and their association included Jackson spending time at Trump properties, such as Trump Tower and the Trump Taj Mahal. There are accounts of them spending time together, and Trump has spoken about their relationship, claiming to have "known Michael Jackson very well." Jackson also spent time with the Trump children.

Notably, Trump publicly defended Jackson during the period of child molestation allegations.

Trump expressed his belief in Jackson's innocence, which was a form of public support during a time when Jackson was facing intense media scrutiny and public condemnation.

Trump has spoken positively of Jackson's character and talent, describing him as a "genius" and "an amazing guy." He also spoke about Jackson as a very smart businessman.

It's important to remember that their association occurred before Trump's entry into politics.

Also, it is important to remember the complexity of Michael Jackson's life.

In essence, their relationship involved a degree of personal acquaintance and, significantly, public support from Trump during Jackson's legal troubles.

Sources:

Donald Trump Jr. on Playing with Michael Jackson as a Kid and the 'Shock' of Abuse Allegations - People.com

 people.com

Donald Trump - Michael Jackson 1958 - 2009 - Videos Index on TIME.com

content.time.com

Michael Jackson Wanted to Kiss Melania Trump to Make Donald Trump Jealous - IMDb

 www.imdb.com

The relationship between Donald Trump and Mike Tyson has a long and complex history, marked by both business dealings and personal support. Donald Trump played a significant role in promoting some of Mike Tyson's fights, particularly those held at his Atlantic City casinos. This established a strong business association between the two. There are also records of Trump acting as an advisor to Tyson in earlier parts of Tysons' career. When Mike Tyson faced legal troubles and subsequent incarceration in the 1990s, Donald Trump publicly offered support.

Notably, Trump made a controversial proposal that would have allowed Tyson to potentially avoid prison time by contributing a portion of his fight earnings to victims of rape and abuse. Trump also publicly stated his belief that Tyson was "railroaded" in his court case.

Their relationship has continued over the years. Mike Tyson has also publicly voiced his support for Donald Trump. It is important to understand that the relationship has had many facets, and some of the actions of Donald Trump, where seen as self-serving by many media outlets. Donald Trump's support for Mike Tyson extended beyond mere friendship, involving active attempts to influence Tyson's legal situation. It is also important to understand that the relationship between the two men has been viewed as controversial by many people.

Sources:

Did Donald Trump save Mike Tyson's life 30 years ago? Here is the whole story behind the Trump-Tyson friendship - The Economic Times

 m.economictimes.com

The Time Donald Trump Tried to Get Mike Tyson Out of Going to Prison for Rape

 www.motherjones.com

Zeroing in more on the financial aspect of Donald Trump's relationship with Mike Tyson involves several layers, extending beyond simple friendship. Donald Trump played a significant role

in promoting Mike Tyson's boxing matches, particularly those held at his casinos in Atlantic City. This involved substantial financial investment on Trump's part, with the potential for considerable returns. Hosting these high-profile events generated significant revenue for Trump's casinos, not only from ticket sales but also from increased gambling activity. Following a period of financial disputes between Tyson and his then-manager, Donald Trump stepped in to act as an advisor. This role involved financial strategizing and guidance for Tyson. There are reports that Trump helped Tyson navigate legal and financial issues, although the precise financial arrangements of this advisory role are not always clearly detailed. During Tyson's legal troubles, Trump made a controversial proposal that would have involved Tyson contributing a portion of his fight earnings to victims of rape and abuse. While this proposal was not implemented, it highlights Trump's involvement in Tyson's financial affairs during a critical period. It is important to understand that the relationship between the two men had a large business aspect to it. Donald Trump used his business connections and venues to help promote Tysons' career.

In essence, Donald Trump's financial support of Mike Tyson involved both direct promotion of his fights and advisory roles, with the context of those actions taking place within Trump's business dealings.

In the aftermath of the tragic murders of Jennifer Hudson's mother, brother, and nephew in

2008, Donald Trump provided her and some of her family members with accommodation at the Trump International Hotel and Tower in Chicago. Here's a summary of what's reported:

Reports indicate that Donald Trump offered Jennifer Hudson and her family a place to stay at his Chicago hotel during this incredibly difficult time. This provided them with a secure and private environment as they dealt with the devastating loss. The murders were a high-profile and deeply upsetting event, and the need for security and privacy for the Hudson family was paramount. The provision of accommodation by Donald Trump occurred within this context.

According to reports, Donald Trump expressed concern for Jennifer Hudson's well-being and emphasized that they were being "protected well" at his hotel. It's important to note that this act was seen by some as an act of kindness during a time of extreme grief. This event shows a time when Donald Trump showed compassion to someone during a very hard time in their life.

Sources:

The Nicest Things Ever Done or Said By Donald Trump - Pajiba

 www.pajiba.com

NYC Real Estate Developer Protects Celebrity in his Chicago Hotel due to Dangerous War LIke Conditions on Chicago Streets | StreetEasy

 streeteasy.com

When Nelson Mandela was released from prison in 1990, he planned a tour of the United States to thank Americans for supporting the anti-apartheid movement.

Robben Island legendary prison which held Nelson Mandela

With Ntoza former prisoner with Nelson Mandela on Robben Island which he now gives tours.

At the time, no major airline or high-profile supporter would offer or make available a private jet to accommodate Mandela's tight, multi-city schedule. The Mandela team negotiated with many private jet airlines and the U.S. government to no avail, in steps Donald Trump.

Donald Trump made available one of his private jets (from Trump Air) to personally transport Nelson Mandela and his team across the country.

He did this without fanfare, it wasn't blasted in the media, and Trump didn't try to take public credit for it.

Mandela's team accepted, and the Trump jet helped him travel to important appearances in cities like New York, Boston, and Washington, D.C. Trump made available to rent one of his planes when no one else would, even the U.S. government. It allowed Mandela to reach millions of Americans during a critical time for South Africa's new future. Very few people ever heard about it because Trump did not publicize it himself.

Judge Joe Brown has publicly claimed that Donald Trump engaged in a pattern of lending money to Black business owners and then, in certain instances, refusing to accept repayment of those loans. He has presented this as a form of support or investment in the Black community. Judge Joe Brown has been an unabashed vocal public supporter of Donald Trump and his policies and leadership.

Floyd Mayweather has publicly expressed support for Donald Trump. Floyd Mayweather has made public statements expressing his support for Donald Trump, particularly highlighting Trump's background as a businessman.

He has, in media appearances, given his opinion that Donald Trump was a very good president. He has also been recorded stating that Donald Trump was the best president, in his opinion. A recurring theme in Mayweather's support is his admiration for Trump's business skills. He has emphasized that Trump's experience as a businessman is a key factor in his suitability for leadership. There are reports of Floyd Mayweather attending events that support Donald Trump. Floyd Mayweather has made clear public statements of support for Donald Trump. That support is heavily based on Floyd Mayweather's view of Donald Trump's business skills.

Sources:

"Floyd Mayweather is a sellout coon": Fans react to former boxer Floyd Mayweather's praises for Donald Trump | MMA News - The Times of India

timesofindia.indiatimes.com

<u>Floyd Mayweather praises Trump as the 'best president' and a 'great businessman'</u>

The following are more instances of Donald Trump's historic support of Blacks:

1. Jesse Jackson

In the 1990s, Jesse Jackson praised Trump publicly for hiring minority contractors and supporting economic empowerment initiatives for Black Americans. Trump also supported Jesse Jackson's 1984 presidential campaign.

2. Alveda King (niece of Dr. Martin Luther King Jr.)

She has repeatedly defended Trump against accusations of racism and thanked him for his pro-life support and economic initiatives that benefited Black communities.

3. Robert L. Johnson (Founder of BET)

Johnson, a lifelong Democrat, called Trump's economic policies "great for Black Americans" and said he had to "give Trump credit" for supporting Black businesses.

4. Kanye West

Kanye famously visited Trump in the Oval Office and publicly praised Trump for his work on prison reform and for giving him a platform to speak.

5. Jim Brown (NFL Legend and Civil Rights Activist)

Jim Brown met with Trump and praised him for listening to concerns about criminal justice reform and economic opportunity for Black Americans.

6. Dennis Rodman

Rodman, the NBA star, publicly thanked Trump for helping negotiate relations with North Korea and credited Trump for always treating him fairly.

7. Diamond and Silk (Political Commentators)

They strongly supported Trump throughout his presidency, thanking him for speaking directly to Black Americans and challenging establishment thinking.

8. Jack Brewer (Former NFL Player)

Brewer called Trump "the first Black president we've had in a while" (in spirit) because of how much Trump fought for prison reform and Black economic issues.

9. Alice Johnson (Freed Nonviolent Prisoner)

Alice Marie Johnson has publicly praised Trump repeatedly for personally commuting her sentence and fighting for criminal justice reforms.

10. Van Jones (CNN Analyst)

While very critical of Trump overall, even Van Jones publicly praised Trump for passing the First Step Act, calling it "historic" and "a step toward justice."

11. Herschel Walker (NFL Star)

Herschel Walker, a longtime friend, defended Trump during political attacks, saying Trump was "a champion for all Americans, including Black Americans."

THE BLACK TRUMP SUPPORTER

Meeting the legendary Herschel Walker

12. Snoop Dogg (Early 2000s)

Before politics divided everything, Snoop praised Trump multiple times in the 2000s as a businessman who gave opportunities to everyone, regardless of race. Snoop seems to have come back around to supporting Trump in 2024 after many years of hateful rhetoric.

13. Pastor Darrell Scott

Pastor Scott, a Black church leader, worked directly with Trump on urban revitalization and prison reform policies, calling Trump "the most pro-Black president in recent history."

14. Isaiah Washington (Actor, Grey's Anatomy)

After being "red pilled," Isaiah thanked Trump for giving attention to prison reform and giving Black Americans more political power.

15. Kaya Jones (Singer, former Pussycat Dolls member)

Though not as high-profile, she has publicly credited Trump for "caring deeply about minorities and forgotten communities."

16. Burgess Owens (Congressman, former NFL Player)

Burgess Owens has praised Trump for focusing on Black entrepreneurship and school choice policies benefiting minority communities.

17. Wayne Dupree (Radio Host)

Dupree, a Black conservative media figure, has often said Trump opened doors for conversations about race that politicians were too afraid to touch.

18. Clarence Henderson (Civil Rights Legend)

Henderson, a surviving member of the 1960 Greensboro sit ins, endorsed Trump for his actions that advanced the Black community.

19. Andrew Giuliani's Black Staffers' Testimonies

Many Black staffers who worked in Trump's organization (in real estate and hospitality) have spoken fondly of him, saying he treated minority employees with dignity and fairness.

20. Senator Tim Scott (South Carolina)

Tim Scott worked with Trump on criminal justice reform and opportunity zone policies — and has said Trump "was very engaged" on issues facing Black Americans.

Summary:

While a lot of media focused on division, the real record shows Trump had meaningful and sometimes surprising relationships with many Black leaders, including civil rights veterans, business moguls, athletes, pastors, and cultural figures.

EPILOGUE

(A BRIDGE BUILT OF CONVICTION)

Years in the making, this project, this exploration of a Black Trump supporter's perspective, concludes not with a period but with an ellipsis. It's a pause, a moment of reflection on a journey that defied expectations and challenged preconceptions. To stand proudly, unapologetically, in a space where those two identities, Black and Trump supporters, collided was to navigate a landscape fraught with misunderstanding and, at times, outright hostility.

This wasn't about blind allegiance. It was about a deep-seated belief in the principles that resonated, the policies that offered a different path. It was about recognizing that the narrative, so often painted in broad strokes of monolithic thought, was far more nuanced and complex. It was about claiming the right to individual thought, to challenge the status quo, and to refuse to be confined by the expectations of others.

The years spent crafting this narrative were a testament to the power of conviction. They were a journey through the storm of social and political discourse, a navigation of the fault lines that divide us. It was a process of understanding, of articulating a perspective that often went unheard.

This project was never intended to be a universal representation of Black thought. It was, and remains, a personal testament, a bridge built of conviction across a chasm of division. It's a reminder that within every community, within every demographic, there exists a spectrum of thought, a tapestry of experiences. It's an invitation to listen, to understand, and to recognize the humanity that binds us, even in the face of profound disagreement.

The work does not end here. The conversation continues, and the dialogue evolves. This project is but a single voice in a chorus of many, a contribution to a larger narrative that seeks to understand the complexities of our shared experience. It's a testament to the enduring power of individual conviction, a belief that even in the face of overwhelming odds, a single voice can make a difference.

Paris is for Lovers

With Lynsey enjoying Paris

THE BLACK TRUMP SUPPORTER

Relaxing Strassbourg, France

Repping my record label All Elite Music on the amazing Table Mountain, Cape Town South Africa

The Black Trump Supporter

Mr. & Mrs.

Michael Ameer

Beautiful Cape Town, SA

THE BLACK TRUMP SUPPORTER

My crew & record label All Elite Music at my wedding!

Burg Khalifa, Dubai, UAE

Lynsey enjoying the German tradition of Oktoberfest!

Acknowledgments

I would like to thank Jordan Farley, editor of the Populist Wire online political magazine, who gave me the push to start this momentous undertaking and to be a contributor. Jordan is super dedicated to this cause, and I am there with him every step of the way.

A "BIG SHOUT OUT" also goes to Dr. William Steiner and his wife, who motivated me to edit my initial drafts of the book. Dr. Steiner is an author of over 10 books, a pilot, a veteran, a martial arts master, a dentist and editor of The Populist Wire and an all-around superhuman being. He also motivated me to take on this project and has graciously written the foreword.

To my beautiful wife, Lynsey Jodi Schaefer-Williams, thank you for continuing to kick me in the ass to finish this long-delayed and overdue project. I may have slowed down but I never gave up. Your love and support are greatly appreciated.

A very special thank you to Ms. Lindy Li. Lindy has given me an "ALL ACCESS PASS" to the Harris / Walz campaign and the Biden Administration (as a prolific fundraiser). This is priceless for a political pundit and author. Having a front-row seat to the inner workings of the most consequential election of our time is amazing. Lindy, being a Democrat who has helplessly watched as the party moved away from her and working-class people, has the most interesting perspective that speaks to the heart of this endeavor. And a special mention goes to Patrick Bet-David whose hugely successful podcast connected me to Ms. Li.

James Golden, aka Mr. Snerdley (author, talk radio show producer and partner to Rush Limbaugh), you and Rush Limbaugh have hugely impacted my transition to a big, card-carrying, unapologetic, staunch conservative. Your contributions and success in radio will go down in history as unmatched. There is a noticeable gaping hole in conservative punditry that can never be replaced. Rest In Power "RUSH LIMBAUGH"!

There is an old saying, "We will sell no wine, before it's time". Though delayed, this project comes right after the biggest political comeback and earthquake in the history of the United States (MAGA!). So, theoretically it's right on time.

www.ingramcontent.com/pod-product-compliance
Lightning Source LLC
Chambersburg PA
CBHW060946050426
42337CB00052B/1538